Failures in
Group Work

Robert K. Conyne

Failures in Group Work

How We Can Learn From Our Mistakes

SAGE Publications
International Educational and Professional Publisher
Thousand Oaks   London   New Delhi

For information:

SAGE Publications, Inc.
2455 Teller Road
Thousand Oaks, California 91320
E-mail: order@sagepub.com

SAGE Publications Ltd.
6 Bonhill Street
London EC2A 4PU
United Kingdom

SAGE Publications India Pvt. Ltd.
M-32 Market
Greater Kailash I
New Delhi 110 048 India

Printed in the United States of America

Library of Congress Cataloging-in-Publication Data

Conyne, Robert K.
    Failures in group work: How we can learn from our mistakes /
by Robert K. Conyne.
        p. cm.
    Includes bibliographical references and index.
    ISBN 0-7619-1289-4 (hardcover: alk. paper)
    ISBN 0-7619-1290-8 (pbk.: alk. paper)
    1. Group counseling. 2. Group psychotherapy. 3. Group counseling—
Case studies. 4. Group psychotherapy—Case studies. I. Title.
    BF637.C6 C5717 1999
    158'.35—dc21   98-40210

This book is printed on acid-free paper.

99 00 01 02 03 04 05 7 6 5 4 3 2 1

Acquisition Editor:	Jim Nageotte/Kassie Gavrilis
Editorial Assistant:	Heidi Van Middlesworth
Production Editor:	Wendy Westgate
Editorial Assistant:	Nevair Kabakian
Typesetter:	Lynn Miyata
Cover Designer:	Candice Harman
Indexer:	Molly Hall

Contents

Acknowledgments

Thanks, first and foremost, to those groups and members of them who have provided the "grist for the mill" that went into the production of this book.

I am appreciative of the University of Cincinnati for granting the sabbatical that allowed me to devote more concerted time to this effort.

Thanks to my brother, John Conyne, for his inspired Garpp cartoons and to Bruce Bean for his technical assistance; to my son, Zachary, for his primary work on the "Group Work Rainbow"; to my daughter, Suzanne, for her valuable computer virtuosity and assistance; and to my wife, Lynn, for her forbearance and helpful critique of my work during this time.

Finally, kudos to Jim Nageotte, from Sage, for his helpful guidance and support and to the reviewers of this book whose preproduction comments were so helpful.

Introduction

THE MAKINGS OF A GROUP WORK FAILURE

The new group leader excitedly wrote in his session-by-session journal that the opening session had been a triumph! He reported that members had jumped right in without any apparent hesitancy at all. They had begun to divulge personal experiences and to give each other frank feedback. Nearly all of them had agreed on the group goals that the leader explained. They had all seemed to understand confidentiality and had accepted the group rules provided by the leader. One member had disclosed her deep fear of being in groups, and two others had tried to reassure her that this group would be very different. Another member had cried while telling the group about his infidelity. The energy level had been very high, and it had been almost as if the group just went right into the working stage. The leader was sure that this group was going to be not only a breeze to run but a wonderfully exciting experience for everyone, even for the one member who had been silent throughout. So, for the second session, the group leader planned to pick up where they had left off and to try to promote deeper interaction.

The second session, however, was markedly different. The silent member did not return, and the others seemed very quiet, maybe resistive. When they did talk, they tended to question the group goals and rules. Some wondered if this was the right group for them. The session was a painful one for the leader, and he wondered if anyone would return for the next one. He became fearful that the group was going to fail and hoped his supervisor could help him sort this out. We will return to this situation later.

THE PREMISE OF THIS BOOK

This book is about failure in group work and how leaders can learn from mistakes they have made. Of course, group work leadership provides ample opportunity to fail. We will examine a variety of failure examples throughout this book and, importantly, how leaders were able to transform mistakes into successes.

Most articles and texts in any area of specialization, group work being no different, contain material about successful ventures. Consider two examples. Research studies that find no statistical significance rarely are published in scholarly journals, and group work textbooks describe techniques and strategies that are known to be generally effective. All this is as it should be, for readers need to discover what works. However, it is the thesis of this book that processing mistakes and failures in group work can lead to substantially important learning and that readers can benefit from reading about them.

There is plenty of everyday evidence to support this idea that mistakes can be turned to advantage. Here are some illustrations.

At my 11-year-old son's fifth-grade "graduation" ceremony, the principal wryly observed to the audience that even these successful graduates had each known some failure along the way. She went on to define failure as the opportunity to do things differently. She suggested that people can learn as much from a wrong answer as from a right one. In a television commercial for a major sporting goods company, Michael Jordan, the acclaimed basketball player, confessed that he had failed over and over again in his life and that this was why he had succeeded. He gave an example from the basketball court, where he said he had missed thousands of shots, lost hundreds of games, and missed the game-winning shot many times. Fran Tarkenton, a National Football League Hall of Fame quarterback, said in his book *What Losing Taught Me About Winning* that we need not be destroyed by failures; rather, we can accept them and evolve, as life is built on mistakes. He reminded readers to remember how many times they fell off their bike before learning to ride (cited in McCafferty, 1997).

It is common knowledge, if not folklore, that many other famous people arose from the ashes of apparent failure and defeat: Isaac Newton was a poor performer in grade school; Walt Disney was fired from a newspaper for lack of ideas; Beethoven's teacher branded him to be without hope as a composer; Babe Ruth struck out 1,330 times but hit 714 home runs; and Einstein's teacher thought him to be a slow thinker, unsociable, and lost interminably in daydreams (Canfield & Hansen, 1993).

There is an important relationship between failure and success. Scott Adams, creator of the famous cartoon character Dilbert, provided a key to this relationship when he said, "Everything I've done that's good is based on some other failure. Of course, none of this losing would be fun if it was all I did" (Brothers, 1997, p. 14).[1] To fail is just not pleasurable or rewarding. And if people failed over and over again, with no learning and no change, then this would be a kind of continuing hell.

Of critical importance in converting failure to success is the capacity to learn and to try again, this next time with more wisdom. In his short story about pool, Dolan (1998) has the pool instructor cautioning his student not to hate a missed shot and not to rush to shoot the next one, but rather to accept misses as part of the game, providing the important opportunity to figure out what was done wrong. Closer to home, Hicks and Peterson (1997) pointed out, in their insightful analysis of "half-truths" and "real truths" in human development, that it is but a "half-truth" to believe that people learn from their failures. As they observe, "It is not the pain or failure in themselves that have value, it's the stopping and thinking" (p. 182). The "real truth," these authors indicated, is that people learn when they examine their experiences, asking themselves these questions: "What worked? What didn't work? What do I want to do differently the next time?" (p. 182).

Failure is a part of being alive, a part of the human condition. I have made innumerable mistakes and have failed many times. For example, I can to this day immediately, vividly, and painfully recall an event that happened in my childhood. I was an 8-year-old Cub Scout. Our troop was putting on a talent show. The audience was packed with proud parents and family members. I had prepared the song "The Little White Cloud That Cried," which had been sung in a uniquely outrageous style by a popular singer at the time by the name of Johnny Ray. I was prepared, and my rehearsals went well. Once I got "on stage," however, all I could focus on was a man who seemed to me to have a very large head and who was sitting right in the middle of the audience. He seemed to stare harshly and disapprovingly at me. The message I created for myself was "Kid, you will never do it!" Consumed with this thought, I froze and was unable to sing a single word! I was humiliated.

Indeed, this was a failure experience. But I learned from it. Looking back, although I did not know what "processing" was, that is what I did afterwards, however crudely as a youngster. I figured out that the event was just that—a one-time trial—and that I should not allow it to govern me in the future. Consequently, subsequent performance trials went better. Now, although I do not perform as a singer or an impersonator, I am required as a professor and program director to perform by presenting material to others daily, giving lectures, workshops, and conference presentations, and by leading meetings. I use my talent show failure experience to help me not only to be prepared but also to focus my attention on delivering my message instead of being overly concerned that others are judging me.

Just as in the various examples cited above, leaders can correct what has not gone well in a group and turn apparent failure into success. But to do this, they must be able to learn from their mistakes. This is the basic premise of this book.

TURNING FAILURE TO SUCCESS IN GROUP WORK

Let us now return to the opening case situation, as the leader meets with his supervisor. What went wrong? Sometimes group leaders misinterpret events. This is what happened in our example. The group leader's judgment of the initial session was unduly rosy, missing the importance of group development. Members were not ready to move forward, and they could be expected to retreat somewhat in the next session. A second mistake, made during Session 2, was for the leader to become caught up in a fear that the group was failing, a very incapacitating thought. Reaching out to his supervisor for assistance represented a good choice.

The supervisor was able to point out that the early disclosure and feedback that occurred in Session 1 were both too much and too intense for what the group and its members were prepared for in that first session. They got ahead of themselves developmentally. As well, the members too readily accepted the group goals and rules that the leader laid out for them. The member who did not speak may not have ever felt included or attended to, perhaps having been crowded out by the expressions of others. And after a week had gone by between sessions, it would have been a good idea to check with members at the start of the next session to assess their present thoughts and feelings.

After considering and discussing these points in supervision, the leader decided on a different strategy for approaching the third session: He would begin to consistently check with members about their thoughts, ideas, and feelings before moving ahead. That is, he would try being more of a collaborative leader and would then monitor the effectiveness of this approach.

This change demonstrates how a leader can begin to learn from his mistakes and, in so doing, can turn failure into success. It also shows how a supervisor can help a group leader to review and process events and experiences, putting them into an explanatory conceptual framework that allows for taking corrective action steps.

FORMAT OF THE BOOK

Chapter 1, "A Framework for Examining Group Work," presents the framework for examining group work that will be used throughout the book. It describes and gives examples of comprehensive group work, drawing from the Association for Specialists in Group Work (ASGW) *Professional Standards for the Training of Group Workers* (ASGW, 1991), *Comprehensive Group Work: What It Means and How to Teach It* (Conyne, Wilson, & Ward, 1997), and a recent review of the ASGW training standards that offers refined definitions of the four group work types: task groups, psychoeducation groups, counseling groups, and psychotherapy groups (Conyne & Wilson, 1998). Core competencies that need to be mastered by all group work leaders are summarized. Relatively more space is devoted to best practices in group work and their organizing principles, the "3 P's" of group work leadership: "planning, performing, and processing" (ASGW, 1998; Rapin & Conyne, in press).

Chapters 2 through 9 contain case studies drawn from my experience as a group leader, supervisor, teacher, and researcher. Each illustrates how group leaders were confronted with challenging situations and how they responded. Mistakes are made and, in most cases, recovered from successfully.

Though the case situations are all drawn from actual experiences with groups, I have tried to conceal or alter descriptions, without losing substance, in order to protect identities. In some instances, I have amalgamated information to produce disguised descriptions. It would be inaccurate to assume that any case accurately represents any character or situation.

Two chapters are devoted to each of the four group work types: task, psychoeducation, counseling, and psychotherapy. Specific functions of group leadership—planning, performing, and processing—are emphasized in each of the chapters. Finally, each chapter is concluded with an "Analysis" section and "Questions for Reflection and Discussion."

Use the analysis of each case to help you relate the example to larger group work issues associated with "Best Practices in Group Work" and with group work competencies. Also, allow the various case analyses to stimulate your thinking about understanding each case. Use the "Questions for Reflection and Discussion" to provide concrete opportunities for you to deepen your understandings of group work and of how you can apply it. If you are a student in a class or a workshop trainee, it also may be helpful to discuss your responses to these questions with other learners.

Chapters 2 and 3 address task groups. These groups are conducted to improve performance or production by members of such work units as committees, classes, task forces, and planning teams.

In Chapter 2, "Developing a Group Program," two young staff members from a prestigious but traditional mental health center compare notes about problems facing the agency. They determine that the service modality typically used, individual counseling, needs to be complemented by introduction of a group work program. Their attempt to lead a clinical staff meeting to begin work on program development is painfully unsuccessful. Discussion with their supervisor reveals the importance of planning (the first "P" of group leadership) before group meetings and how the leaders might have improved the group meeting through fuller attention to planning.

In Chapter 3, "The Task Group Leader Should Not Deliver Group Counseling," the university counselor is asked to chair a universitywide task force on substance abuse prevention. Unresolved personal issues of the counselor are touched off by the experiences of a task force member. In addition, the counselor chooses the only leadership style that she knows, drawn from person-centered group counseling. The task force nearly disbands. This experience illustrates the importance of performance (the second "P") by showing how a more appropriate leadership model would have provided a better fit.

Chapters 4 and 5 are concerned with psychoeducation groups. These groups use a semistructured format to develop knowledge and skills to solve or prevent problems.

In Chapter 4, "Missing the Driving Force," the leader focuses exclusively on delivering content, forgetting completely about process. This mistake commonly occurs in psychoeducation groups. Processing (the third "P" of group leadership) in this case underlines the importance of the "driving force" of all group work—process. Once this force is rediscovered, failure is avoided in subsequent sessions of the group.

Chapter 5, "Lacking a Plan," demonstrates that psychoeducation groups need to be planned carefully in advance. In this instance, the lack of a plan left the leaders in a lurch for the first two sessions. Planning (the first "P") helped them to correct the mistake and develop the intentional structure necessary for moving the group ahead productively.

Chapters 6 and 7 focus on counseling groups. These groups use interpersonal problem-solving approaches to help members move ahead with their lives.

Group leaders can never be certain of what is going to occur in their group, even though good developmental models exist. In Chapter 6, "Surprise and Challenge in Group Leadership," the fundamental principle of confidentiality is inadvertently compromised in a counseling group focusing on issues of spirituality, resulting in a serious threat to the group's continuation. By attending to performance (the second "P") in this case, the group leaders are able to work with the members to "turn around" the group.

In Chapter 7, "Violating the Code," action taken by group leaders to remove a member from the counseling group for trainees violates the perceived collaborative culture that the leaders and group members worked hard to achieve. After the group members nearly revolt in the next session, the leaders are able to salvage the group and help make the incident a critically important one for growth. Processing (the third "P") is shown to be especially important in this experience.

Chapters 8 and 9 address psychotherapy groups. These groups focus on individuals, using the group process to produce significant psychological and/or emotional change.

Attention to diversity and multicultural issues is an important part of all group work, including group psychotherapy. In many ways, group work is synonymous with diversity. In Chapter 8, "Problems With Diversity," the coleaders are confronted with the relationship between diversity and dissonance and how cohesion always needs to be a focus. In addition, they (and all African Americans) are confronted with a withering racist attack by a group member, the intensity of which threatens the group's existence. The strength demonstrated by group members is an important healing factor in this case, and the planning function is shown to be especially important.

Managed care is affecting all health care, including group therapy. Chapter 9, "You Need to Trust the Process," focuses on growing influences associated with managed care: brief, structured, outcome-oriented group therapy, where the leader assumes a more active role. Experimentation with these influences by a therapy group leader is examined in relation to how he fails to continue giving attention to process, thereby showing the importance of the performance function.

The final chapter, "Learning From Our Mistakes Through Processing," summarizes the importance of the 3 P's in leading effective task, psychoeducation, counseling, and therapy groups. Specific attention is given to between-session processing, and its five steps: transpose, reflect, discover, apply, and evolve. Distinctions are made between pragmatic processing and deep processing, and the importance of both is emphasized.

The book concludes with an unexamined case situation, to which readers are invited to apply the five steps of processing as they seek to turn a potential group work failure into a success.

NOTE

1. Used with permission from the Cincinnati Enquirer/Perry Brothers.

I dedicate this book to all of us who, at far too many times,
imagine that we have failed in our group work, or
that we are surely about to, given how things have gone so far.
May the cases of this book show how we can
learn from our groups, improve our skills, and take steps
to prevent failures from occurring in the first place.

PART I

Theoretical Framework

CHAPTER 1

A Framework for Examining Group Work

CHAPTER PURPOSE

As explained in the Introduction, this book is intended to show how mistakes and apparent failure in group work can be turned to advantage by knowledgeable and skilled group work leaders. With the exception of this first and the last chapters, all chapters present detailed case examples of how leaders can successfully cope with negative events and experiences. This chapter is intended to introduce several basic principles of group work. These principles are presented before the case examples because they will be important for later analysis of the cases. Now let us turn to considering the group work framework to be drawn from throughout this book.

GROUPS ARE ALL AROUND US

Groups are part of most people's daily lives in Western society (Gladding, 1995). Despite the cultural heritage in the United States of individualism and independence and the emerging emphasis on computer use, it is virtually impossible to conduct one's personal or work life without encountering group life. Beginning with birth, most of us are born into a family group, are socialized and formally educated through a variety of group experiences, work with colleagues, and participate in volunteer, religious, or recreational opportunities that involve others. It is accurate to state that most people in our society are "group beings."

GROUP WORK METHODS PERTINENT
TO COUNSELORS AND OTHER HELPERS

Due to their omnipresence, groups serve as important influencers of personal growth and development. Interpersonal experiences in groups are a primary source of learning about ourselves and each other. Entire psychological disciplines (social psychology), theories of personality development (e.g., Sullivan, 1953), and theories of group psychotherapy (e.g., Yalom, 1995) are based on the importance and power of interpersonal and group relations.

Group Counseling and Group Psychotherapy

For counselors and other helpers, the group historically has provided a method of therapeutic change, most notably through group counseling and group psychotherapy. Clinical and counseling psychology, counseling, and social work programs include group counseling and psychotherapy training within their educational requirements. A supporting and extensive body of literature devoted to these group therapeutic applications has been developed in the latter half of this century (e.g., Corey, Corey, Callanan, & Russell, 1992; Gazda, 1989; Gladding, 1995; Jacobs, Harvill, & Masson, 1994; Trotzer, 1989; Yalom, 1995).

Practitioners are being increasingly expected to deliver group counseling and psychotherapy in mental health and social service agencies of all kinds. This expanding demand is due to a realization that group counseling and group psychotherapy are effective means for resolving psychological problems and dysfunction (e.g., Seligman, 1995; Spitz, 1996) and to the managed-care industry's pressure for cost-effective treatment interventions (Cummings, 1995).

Other Group Work Methods:
Psychoeducation and Task Groups

Counselors and other helpers have begun to realize increasingly that other group methods besides group counseling and group psychotherapy can be used to produce intended change. During this last decade, new attention has been given to using semistructured group procedures to educate and teach skills (psychoeducation groups) and to employing group approaches for improving productivity and performance in work settings (task groups). Thus, the range of group applications available for counselors and other helpers to use has expanded, a trend that can be expected to continue into the next millennium (Conyne, 1985).

COMPREHENSIVE GROUP WORK

Group Work

Contemporary counselors and other helpers are becoming oriented toward group work as an organizing construct. As defined by the Association for Specialists in Group Work (ASGW, 1991), group work is

> a broad professional practice that refers to the giving of help or the accomplishment of tasks in a group setting. It involves the application of group theory and process by a capable professional practitioner to assist an interdependent collection of people to reach their mutual goals, which may be personal, interpersonal, or task-related in nature. (p. 14)

As indicated within the above definition, group work is a comprehensive professional practice (Conyne, Wilson, & Ward, 1997). The "group work tent" is broad and encompassing, holding room for a wide variety of applications. In the ASGW *Professional Standards for the Training of Group Workers* (1991), this comprehensive span of applications is categorized into four methods or specializations that are consistent with the earlier discussion in this chapter: (a) task groups, (b) psychoeducation groups, (c) counseling groups, and (d) psychotherapy groups. These group work types, and the core competencies common to them, are graphically depicted by the "Group Work Rainbow" (Figure 1.1). The Rainbow suggests the simultaneous independence and interdependence of the group work types and the core competencies that are germane to all group work.

Core Competencies

Regardless of the type of group they may lead, group leaders must first master a set of core competencies. These core competencies provide group work leaders with a foundation of group work knowledge and skills. Examples of core knowledge include understanding principles of group dynamics, the therapeutic elements of groups, ethical issues applied to group work, and the differences among group work types. Core skills needed by group workers include being able to open and close

Figure 1.1. The Group Work Rainbow
SOURCE: Zachary Conyne-Rapin, Suzanne Conyne-Rapin, and Robert Conyne. Used by permission.

sessions, encourage participation of members, and model effective group leader behavior (ASGW, 1991). Mastery of the core competencies precedes learning the knowledge and skills for conducting any of the four group work types.

Group Work Types

With additional focused training and supervision counselors can be prepared to deliver the four types of group work shown in Figure 1.1. The ASGW training standards define and set forth advanced competencies associated with task, psychoeducation, counseling, and psychotherapy groups. A brief discussion of the four group work types follows (ASGW, 1991; Conyne, 1989; Conyne & Wilson, 1998; Conyne, Wilson, & Ward, 1997).

Task Groups. Task groups are conducted to enhance or resolve performance and production goals in work groups. The task group leader functions as a facilitator, using group collaborative problem solving, team building, program development consultation, and/or system change strategies (Conyne, Rapin, & Rand, 1997; Conyne & Wilson, 1998). For example, such a leader might help an employee assistance staff develop its strategic plan for the next 5 years.

Psychoeducation Groups. Psychoeducation groups feature transmission, discussion, and integration of factual information and skill building through the use of semistructured exercises and group process. The goal is to educate members or develop their skills, and the leader functions as a trainer and facilitator (Brown, 1997; Conyne & Wilson, 1998; Ettin, Heiman, & Kopel, 1988). For example, such a leader might help outpatient group members understand and develop specific assertion skills.

Counseling Groups. Counseling groups are conducted by group counselors to improve coping with problems of living by focusing on interpersonal problem solving, interactive feedback, and support methods within a here-and-now framework (Conyne & Wilson, 1998; Trotzer, 1989). For example, a counseling group leader might help a group of adolescents in their adaptation to family and school demands.

Psychotherapy Groups. Psychotherapy groups are conducted by group therapists to reduce psychological and/or emotional dysfunction through exploration of the antecedents to current behavior, using intrapersonal and interpersonal assessment, diagnosis, and interpretation and by connecting historical material with the present (Conyne & Wilson, 1998; Yalom, 1995; a brochure of the American Group Psychotherapy Association, 1995, entitled *A Consumer's Guide to Group Psychotherapy,* may also prove useful). For example, a psychotherapy group leader might help inpatient group members to manage their mood disorders more effectively.

BEST PRACTICES IN GROUP WORK

Each of the four group work types demands special advanced competencies. Together with the core competencies, their mastery contributes substantially to the group work leader's capacity to deliver what has become known as "best practices in group work." "Best practices in group work refer to those activities, strategies, and interventions that are consistent and current with effective and appropriate professional, ethical, and community standards" (Rapin & Conyne, in press).

Our presentation of best practices in group work is based on ASGW's *Ethical Guidelines for Group Counselors* (1989), ASGW's *Professional*

Standards for the Training of Group Workers (1991), and the American Counseling Association (ACA) *Code of Ethics and Standards of Practice* (1995). The work is consistent, as well, with the ongoing developments of the ASGW Ethics Committee. This committee, cochaired by Lynn Rapin and Linda Keel, has produced a new document, *Association for Specialists in Group Work Best Practice Guidelines* (ASGW, 1998), which is included in the Appendix. This document was recently approved by the ASGW Executive Board to replace ASGW's *Ethical Guidelines.*

Best practice guidelines can be organized into the "3 P's" of group work leadership: planning, performing, and processing (Conyne, Smith, & Wathen, 1997; Rapin & Conyne, in press). Planning, performing, and processing are cyclical functions that group work leaders need to engage in with every type of group and, usually, in every session of each group. The following brief discussion of planning, performing, and processing adapts and expands the work of Rapin and Conyne (in press).

Planning

In planning, group work leaders address all steps before conducting the initial group session. Relatively little attention in group leader training and supervision is given to this important function. In fact, not so long ago, it was believed by many (some to this day) that if group leaders were "really good," not only did they not need to plan, but planning would detract from their spontaneity and effectiveness as group leaders. Today it is considered best practice for group leaders to plan thoroughly before the first group session or meeting is held.

Also, it is essential that any groups being offered under sponsorship of an agency or other organization be consistent with the mission of the setting and have the full permission and support of the mission administrative personnel. Obtaining such support requires the application of excellent planning skills.

Current understanding of best practices in planning includes the following.

Be Aware of Professional Context. Group leaders need to understand and abide by the relevant code of ethics in the profession and comply with applicable licensure, certification, and accreditation standards. As well, group leaders need to behave in accord with community standards. Groups provided under organizational sponsorship must be consistent with the organizational mission and be supported by its decision makers.

When developing a program of group services, securing participation and support of agency personnel is vital.

Develop Conceptual Underpinnings. Group leaders need to value group work as a potent and effective vehicle for growth and change and to help group members (and colleagues) to appreciate it. They should be able to define the type of group they are using and to operate within their scope of practice. Possessing a coherent conceptual framework and effectively applying it to their work are important.

Conduct an Ecological Assessment. Groups must emerge from and directly address the needs and press of the local community. It is necessary to assess community and population needs, with particular attention to multicultural factors, and to match these needs with an appropriate group work type.

Implement Program Development and Evaluation Principles. Group goals, themes, and activities must be consistent with the ecological assessment of community needs. A group plan should be produced that clearly elucidates group work type, purpose, conceptual framework, methods, strategies, member recruitment and selection, leader qualifications, evaluation methods, and a session-by-session outline (see Conyne, Wilson, & Ward, 1997, for examples).

Identify Resources for Managing the Group Program. Coleadership of groups is recommended by many experts. Although clear advantages accrue to this approach, selection and matching of leaders must be done with care, giving attention to diversity, compatibility, and competency. For instance, in terms of diversity, it is generally desirable for a man and woman to co-lead groups (an exception might be gay and lesbian groups) because this model provides expanded opportunities for identification and modeling to occur. In all coleadership situations, the leaders need to attend closely to their continuing working relationship—their group work leadership is a direct outgrowth of it.

In terms of marketing and recruiting of the group experience, leaders must secure appropriate meeting space and supportive backup resources, develop procedures for client payment of any fees that may be involved (e.g., insurance considerations), and decide to use a solo or a coleadership model.

Develop a Professional Disclosure Statement. Group leaders should prepare a printed professional disclosure statement. This document, which is often required by licensure statute, can be used to inform prospective group members about the group leader(s)' training, experience, licensing, fees for service, and specific qualifications for offering the group.

Prepare the Group and Its Members. Research shows that pregroup member preparation for counseling and therapy groups significantly contributes to productive group experiences (Yalom, 1995). Generalizing this approach to task and psychoeducation groups would seem to be a sound idea. Screening of prospective members for the group needs to be conducted in counseling and in psychotherapy groups and, as appropriate, in the other group types. It is essential that confidentiality and its limits be explained to members of counseling and psychotherapy groups and, as appropriate, in psychoeducation and task groups. Obtaining informed consent from members regarding all aspects of the planned group is essential.

Pursue Professional Development. Group leaders need to regularly revitalize their knowledge and skills through continuing education, reading, attendance at professional meetings, research and writing, and other appropriate pursuits, consistent with licensure and certification requirements. An example of an important developing area for all group practitioners to address through professional development is diversity, which was discussed above.

Be Aware of Trends and Technological Changes. Group leaders need to scan societal change for trends, technological advancements, and any other emerging matters that may influence group work. Managed care and its effects on mental health practice, the changing demographic complexion of this country, and rapid technological changes involving computer applications all represent such influencing factors.

Performing

In performing, group work leaders are concerned with all that occurs within the actual group sessions. Performing is the most studied of the three functions, and it receives most of the attention in training and supervision. After all, performing has to do with ongoing group life and how the leaders contribute to it.

Current understanding of best practices in performing includes the following.

Know Thyself. As various experts have noted, the most important performance factor is the ability of group leaders to integrate their natural strengths in their work (e.g., Corey, 1995; Corey & Corey, 1997; Trotzer, 1989). To do this, leaders must be aware of what they do well and also of their limitations.

Effectively Deliver Group Competencies. In addition to using themselves as an instrument of growth and change, group leaders need to master the core competencies of group work and the advanced competencies associated with the type of group work that they are providing. A combination of knowledge, skills, and supervised practice is necessary for developing competence. See the earlier discussion in this chapter for more detail.

Adapt the Group Plan. Group leadership involves using professional judgment to adapt the group plan to emerging and changing group situations. The group plan itself is rarely applied without change. Group leaders must be able to modify it, as warranted, within the ongoing delivery of service (Conyne, Wilson, & Ward, 1997).

Master Therapeutic Dynamics and Conditions. Group leaders need to become adept at understanding group development, making and responding to process observations, and harnessing therapeutic conditions. Using a model of group development (e.g., Jones, 1973; Trotzer, 1989) can help leaders to anticipate generally future occurrences and to be ready for making appropriate adaptations as necessary. Making and responding to process observations (e.g., Hanson, 1972) during group sessions or meetings can help leaders to keep the group focused. Harnessing therapeutic conditions, such as cohesion, can serve to drive the group forward productively (Yalom, 1995).

Choose Appropriate Interventions. What group leaders do during sessions needs to be intentional. They should be able to select from a repertoire of options those interventions that appear to hold the greatest chance for success.

Attend to the Here and Now and to Meaning Attribution. Helping members in counseling and psychotherapy groups to relate to events and experiences that are occurring in the present and paying attention to their meaning are the types of interactions that generally are associated with the highest therapeutic value (Yalom, 1995). Applications of this guideline to task and psychoeducation groups require appropriate attention to situational demands.

Collaborate With Members. Though it is sometimes necessary, in times of high distress or crisis, for group leaders to make decisions independently for a member or the group, it is generally preferred that leaders work collaboratively with members in reaching decisions and setting goals. Developing an equal partnership between leaders and members in which the respective expertise of both parties is recognized helps to promote cohesion, interdependence, and productivity.

Include Evaluation. Evaluation is often ignored by group leaders. However, without data, effectiveness cannot be determined. Though it always has been important to include outcome and process evaluation whenever possible, today's increased emphasis on accountability has made evaluation and research even more necessary for group workers. A recent special issue of the *Journal for Specialists in Group Work* (Riva & Kolodner, 1998) on group work research elucidates many important factors related to conducting group work research.

Reliance on clinical judgment as the sole source of evaluation is no longer the standard of practice. Clinical judgment supplemented by process and outcome measurement is the new standard. A number of assessment instruments appropriate for group work are available, as well as guidelines for the use of such instrumentation (e.g., Burlingame & McCollam, 1998; DeLucia-Waack, 1998; Dies, 1978; MacKenzie & Dies, 1982; Pfeiffer, Heslin, & Jones, 1976). At the least, simple post-session evaluations can be obtained (e.g., Hill, 1969), with results built in to guide subsequent activities.

Especially in group counseling and group therapy, due largely to the influence of managed care on treatment, outcome evaluation has assumed special significance. Credible instruments are available to measure various factors, including member satisfaction (e.g., Client Satisfaction Questionnaire; Attkisson, 1984), interpersonal behavior (e.g., Inventory of Interpersonal Problems; Horowitz, 1990), social roles (e.g., Social Adjustment Scale; Weissman, 1973), group climate (e.g., Group Climate Questionnaire—Short; MacKenzie, 1983, 1997), symptom self-report (e.g., Self-Report Symptom Inventory, SCL-90-R; Derogatis, 1975), personality (e.g., Emotions Profile Index; Plutchick & Kellerman, 1974), member goals (e.g., Target Goals; Battle et al., 1966), and change in outcomes (e.g., Outcome Questionnaire; American Professional Credentialing Services, 1996).

All group workers are advised to consider how assessment and evaluation can be more consistently included in their efforts. For leaders of counseling and therapy groups, however, this recommendation is a requirement.

Value Diversity. Group leaders must promote a group climate that values diversity along the full range of considerations. D'Andrea and Daniels' (1997) acronym of RESPECTFUL is helpful in capturing diversity dimensions: *R*eligious/spiritual identity; *E*thnic identity; *S*exual identity; *P*sychological maturity; *E*conomic class standing; *C*hronological challenges; *T*hreats to one's well being; *F*amily history; *U*nique physical characteristics; and *L*ocation of residence.

As Yalom observed in 1975, groups represent a social microcosm of society. In the ensuing 25 years, the nature of North American society has shifted dramatically to become much more broadly diverse. Not surprisingly, members of our groups are beginning to mirror this variation. Group leaders, therefore, in addition to valuing diversity, must develop multicultural awareness, knowledge, and skills that will allow them to function appropriately and effectively with all members.

Maintain a Constant Ethical Surveillance. Group leaders must be vigilant about the conformity of their practices and of overall group events to ethical principles maintained by the profession. For counselors, the *Code of Ethics and Standards of Practice* of the ACA (1995) is a useful reference, as are the new ASGW best practice guidelines (ASGW, 1998; Rapin & Conyne, in press). Applying a process sensitive to ethical decision making, such as that developed by Forester-Miller and Davis (1995), is advisable.

Processing

In the context of the "3 P's" model, processing involves making sense of experience and applying this learning to future group work leadership, both short and long term. Though processing can occur within group sessions, here its use is restricted to before and after sessions of a group.

Engaging in processing outside group sessions or meetings is critically important. Processing helps leaders to evaluate events and experiences that occurred within sessions, to make sense of them, and to plan and adjust for immediate and future sessions. Too frequently, however, processing is overlooked due to time constraints or a reluctance to openly examine one's work. When coleaders are involved, processing also includes requesting and giving feedback and focusing on the quality of their working relationship.

Current understanding of best practices in processing includes the following.

Consistently Schedule Processing Time. Time for processing events and experiences should be scheduled to occur before and after each group session or meeting. At least to begin with, it is wise to consider a general formula for meeting time that is based on the following system: delivery for 2 hours and postprocessing for 2 hours. This 2-hour time block for processing can be divided into two separate meeting times if that is mandated by time demands. Either way, following this approach allows for as much time to be spent on processing as on delivering group services.

Leaders can focus the first hour of processing on examination of the previous session. The second hour then can be spent on considering and making any necessary adjustments in the group plan in preparation for the next session.

Engage in Reflective Practice. Reflective practice ties what group leaders do with its active examination. When group leaders reflect on their practice, they are functioning as action scientists who seek to learn from their experience by identifying what is working and what can be improved (Argyris, Putnam, & Smith, 1987). Information yielded through reflection can then be used to continuously improve future applications.

I suggest that processing involves the group leader's proceeding through five steps, from "pragmatic processing" to "deep processing." These five steps are:

1. *Transpose,* or objectively record events occurring during a session without interpretation or manipulation of the data. This step is related to pragmatic processing.

2. *Reflect,* or infuse subjective experience, such as perceptions, sensations, and values with objective data.

3. *Discover,* or derive learnings and meanings that emerge.

4. *Apply,* or design action strategies for implementation to be tried and tested.

5. *Evolve,* or identify any enduring personal and professional practice principles that might generalize to future group work leading.

Steps 2 through 5 constitute deep processing.

The five steps of processing, as well as pragmatic and deep processing, are discussed more fully in Chapter 10. They are concepts that I have developed, synthesized from previous contributions (Bentz, 1992; Bloom, Engelhart, Furst, Hill, & Krathwohl, 1956; Conyne, 1997; Craik & Lockhart, 1972; Jacobs et al., 1994; Kees & Jacobs, 1990; Rapin & Conyne, in press).

Deep processing (Steps 2-5) may be the least used by group leaders, but I think it holds the most power for learning and change. Following is an example of deep processing drawn from an unnamed supervisee's group journal, with group member names and events disguised:

> At this point, I had to make a decision. I made mental notes of the pragmatic processing events, who said what to whom, what members' reactions were, etc. I then moved into deep processing, and my thoughts went something like this: "Bill seems to be doing some really good work here. He is talking about a painful experience, and it is important to acknowledge his efforts to work on this in the group. I am wondering why Fred said that hostile comment about his mother. . . . His comment and nonverbal signs are not congruent; he does not seem to be a person considering such action. Is Fred manipulating the group? Is he jealous of the attention Bill is getting? How would it be for Fred if I ignore the comment the way the rest of the group had? What's going on with this? What will happen if I do nothing? What are my legal/ethical responsibilities? How am I getting caught up with this?" I decided to wait and see if the mother issue comes up again.

Use Evaluation Data. Leaders must not only evaluate group, member, and leader functioning but also use the resulting data (Patton, 1997). Process data that are collected can inform the leader (and members) about the viability of the group and can be used to help the experience to be targeted to what people need and desire. Outcome data can assist leaders to understand the goal accomplishments of members and overall effectiveness of the group experience.

SUMMARY

This chapter contains a basic framework for understanding some essential aspects of group work. The ubiquitous nature of groups in our society was described, as well as the influence of groups in personal development. A comprehensive conception of group work was presented, encompassing four types of groups that counselors and other helpers can use for growth and change purposes: task, psychoeducation, counseling, and psychotherapy groups. Finally, a current understanding of "best practices in group work" was presented, organized according to the "3 P's" of group work leadership: planning, performing, and processing.

The information contained in this chapter can assist group leaders to be more effective in their work. Moreover, consistent with the theme of this book, knowledge of this information can aid group leaders in converting errors made in their leadership into successful experiences.

We now turn to case examples that demonstrate how group leaders can turn mistakes into advances. Two chapters are devoted to each of the major group work types, beginning with task groups. As well, each chapter highlights the "3 P's" of group work leadership.

Follow along as group work leaders make mistakes, correct them, and learn for the future.

PART II

Task Groups

Cartoon by J. C. Conyne.
Used with permission.

Garpp, the Task Group Leader

Our fearless task group leader, Garpp, makes the egregious error of being a "taskmaster" rather than a task group leader. Very often, leaders of task groups focus exclusively on what is to be produced or accomplished, thereby ignoring the people who are working on this task. Feelings and other important forms of human interaction are assumed to be somehow "off base," detracting from the need to generate output.

Cartoon by J. C. Conyne.
Used with permission.

By committing this mistake, however, task
group leaders actually are unwittingly strip-
ping the group of its power source. Human
interactions and group process serve to drive
a group forward and to keep members involved, satisfied, and productive.

Garpp perhaps should have responded, "Yes,
of course, let's be sure to attend to our feelings, too." By so doing, he would help to
integrate people with work, helping the task
to be accomplished and people to feel good
about themselves and their work.

Cartoon by J. C. Conyne.
Used with permission.

CHAPTER 2

Developing a
Group Program

BACKGROUND

Jason Freed was known from childhood as a "go-getter," a kid who, teachers all agreed, would "go a very long way in life." Besides being blessed with both uncommon intelligence and sensitivity to others, Jason outworked and outhustled just about everyone around him. He was the rare kind of person who knew what he wanted and how to get it, and he was able to do so time and time again without being obnoxious about it or trampling anyone in the process. In fact, Jason was so singularly goal directed that his best friend in high school had dubbed him "O intrepid one."

In addition to his intelligence and focused energy, Jason had learned from his family the value of serving others. His parents, both still working as successful lawyers, were committed to community service and human rights. His father had made a career of representing civil rights cases, and his mother served on the boards of no less than 10 community service agencies in the city. At home, his parents frequently would steer discussions around the dinner table to emphasize values consistent with social service and equality, and Jason and his younger sister had grown up volunteering and working part time at the hospital. Although from a family of means, Jason grew up favoring the "underdog."

After graduating magna cum laude from college, and 3 years after receiving his master's in counseling from an accredited and highly respected training program, Jason Freed returned to his home town. Now 28 years old and not yet married, he was busy garnering the necessary postgraduate supervision hours to become licensed as a clinical counselor in the state. After the big day had come and gone about a year ago, Jason accepted full-time employment as a staff counselor at the Eastland Human Services Center, intending to pour his heart and soul into his new position.

The Eastland Human Services Center was an established private agency located on the fringe of an affluent section of the city. The center employed 15 professional staff drawn from social work, psychology, and psychiatric nursing, along with a consulting psychiatrist. As the counseling profession was a relative "newcomer" in mental health service delivery, Jason was the first counselor to be hired on staff. He was keenly aware of breaking new ground there, not only for himself but also for the profession.

The center long had taken pride in the quality of its clinical staff. Staff were carefully selected, and all fully met necessary credentialing requirements: They had graduated from an accredited program and were licensed in their professional field, and many were certified as specialists. To help clinical staff remain current, the center provided release time and financial support to participate in one (down from two, just in the past year) continuing education program per year. Staff offices and meeting spaces were spacious and attractive. In the regional mental health community, the center was generally recognized as a highly desirable place to work.

In the last 5 years or so, however, the center had begun to be tested in new ways. The primary source of the tension was traceable, most staff agreed (rightly or wrongly), to managed care. Historically, the center had been funded through fee-for-service and indemnity insurance programs held by clients. However, as was the case throughout the region and nationally, the pressure of managed care to control the costs of health and mental health care had begun to have adverse effects on the agency. The general trends were that clients were being seen for fewer individual sessions, a wait list for service had been developed and was becoming ever longer, services were being reimbursed at reduced rates, staff tended to be working more hours to generate necessary revenue, the amount of staff time being spent on case documentation had mushroomed, and communications with or about insurance coverage seemed to take center stage. As one result, for the first time in memory, staff morale at the center had plummeted.

Another source of strain had to do with the center's mission and guiding principles. For the first time, perhaps due to the influence of managed care and the apparent need for change or to the approaching retirements of the agency administrator and director of training, staff were anxious about where the center was headed. Many were beginning to question the orientation of the center on individual, remedial, direct service as being badly out of touch with contemporary needs and realities. Still others staunchly supported the historical legacy of the center, asserting its continued viability.

Having been at the center for only 1 year, Jason was still getting his feet wet. Being the only counselor on staff had been particularly challenging at first. However, with the hire of a second counselor, Sandra Arnold, 3 months earlier, he had automatically felt another kindred spirit and source of professional support. What's more, the decision of staff to make the hire a counselor rather than someone from the more commonly represented professions on staff gave him some concrete assurance that his work as a counselor was being appreciated.

Though initially Jason, like any new staff member, had had his client flow highly controlled by the clinical director, this phase soon passed. Jason's work with individual clients presenting relatively mild concerns was expanded to encompass nearly the full range of diagnoses, and he was loving it. He also had been able to organize case presentations at three clinical staffings and was getting the reputation among staff of being not only highly competent across the board but also an initiator.

At the same time, Jason was becoming increasingly aware of the turmoil that seemed to be brewing among several staff. He too was beginning to feel burdened by what seemed to be the unrelenting procedural demands associated with managed care, and his workload had been getting heavier and heavier during the last few months. He was alarmed when he saw that the client wait list had now exceeded 50, and the new limit cap of 15 on the number of client sessions (though an appeal procedure existed) was grating. He had begun to worry about the effects of all these factors on client service. He thought that talking at least some of this over with Sandra, his counselor colleague, might make some sense.

Since she had joined the staff, Jason had taken Sandra "under his wing," much as Mary Tomlinson, the clinical director known affectionately as "the great compromiser," and one of the most capable therapists Jason had ever met, had initially mentored him. Although both Jason and Sandra were young and single, their relationship was strictly professional. How could it be otherwise these days, given the great attention everyone gave to sexual harassment in the workplace? Besides, they were both far too busy to find the time to get involved in any other way.

They had been going to lunch about three times a week, often with other colleagues. In the past, before joining this staff, Jason had never liked going to lunch, feeling that it took too much time away from his work. His more usual style was either to skip it or to eat a brown-bag lunch at his desk. However, the center culture was such that most staff went out to lunch in small groups, frequenting one of the several bistros and cafes that were but a stone's throw from work. So he had joined in and, to his surprise, had found that he really liked this more relaxed time to spend getting to know other staff, most of whom he enjoyed and respected.

Lately, though, Jason had become aware that lunch discussions were taking a different turn. Where before discussions had been light and fun, full of good humor and sometimes focused on professional issues of interest, now they were becoming somehow darker. Actually, they seemed to reflect the tenor of informal discussions occurring with far greater frequency in the hallways and around the coffeepot at the office.

Concerned, Jason asked Sandra to go to lunch alone, and she accepted. He wanted to sound her out on how she was doing at work, now after nearly 6 months at it. He would listen to her carefully, and if conditions were right, he might try to bounce some of his worries about work off her.

ACTION

Planning

Once seated and settled, Sandra, at Jason's request, began to tell him some of her thoughts about how she was doing. "I love it here, Jason!" she said. "It's the perfect place for me."

Maybe she didn't share any of his concerns, or maybe she was just not willing to say.

"That's wonderful, Sandra. You really have been doing well, I can tell. If there is any way I can be of help, let me know, and I'll try."

The discussion went on in this positive way as they ate, until Jason said, "You know, I have to agree with you about the center; it is a great place. But I've been concerned lately about lots of small things, and they seem to be adding up. You know, stuff like long client wait lists, the mountains of paperwork, and how negative we all seem to be getting, grousing all the time. . . . Does any of this make any sense to you?"

So now the bird had flown out of its cage. Someone else knew of his gathering discontent. Was this the right thing to do? Or would this admission begin to scare a newer staff member?

"You know, I thought maybe it was just me. Yeah, I've noticed some of those things too," she admitted.

They talked some more about their concerns as they returned to work. And they decided to continue their discussion, this time setting aside half an hour a week to do so, drawn from their open time.

Jason and Sandra Identify a Problem. Jason had no idea where these discussions might lead. It was just an opportunity to share and maybe sometimes to cathart. But as they met and began exchanging their impressions of how work was going, they found themselves becoming more task oriented. Of course, for Jason, becoming energized around goals fit his style.

After a couple of meetings, they decided to try identifying clearly what problems existed in the center. They quickly agreed that lowered staff morale due to excessive workload resulting from managed-care requirements was a big one. But, they decided, attributing this problem entirely to a managed-care demon was missing something critically important about the enter itself: Its continued reliance on the provision of individual counseling and therapy as the primary vehicle for service delivery contributed to the overall workload problem for staff and to client waiting lists.

Some others on the staff, they knew, shared this viewpoint, but certainly not all did. This lack of agreement itself posed a problem.

But Jason and Sandra did not know how to address the issue of staff disagreement. Nor did they see it as their role to do so. Instead, they turned to problem solving. In his typical action-oriented way, Jason asked, "What could we do to help the center to improve staff morale and client service?"

Jason and Sandra Develop a Solution. Over time, Jason and Sandra began to cobble together a way to address this problem. In the process, they began to see themselves in the role of change agents. It became clear to them that the center staff needed to find a way to openly address the sources of stress that they were all dealing with but not directly acknowledging. In their view, diminishing staff morale and problems with client service were linked.

They became excited about their discussion, thinking they were on the right track. As they talked further, Jason was able to gradually identify a dissatisfaction with the center about which he had not been fully aware: what he viewed as its traditional, conservative, play-it-safe approach as related to client service. No groups. Minimal community outreach. No consultation. No prevention. He became suddenly aware that here was a litany of deficiencies that needed to be corrected if the center was to survive into the next century. A mission was emerging for him, and Sandra too became caught up in it. But where could all this lead in terms of doing something?

"What we need to do here is to change the delivery system used in the center!" exclaimed Jason, very excitedly. "Otherwise, things are just going to get worse all around."

"Maybe, but the whole thing can't be turned upside down all at once," cautioned Sandra. "That would be impossible and doomed to failure anyway. Let's think about what's more doable."

"Okay, good. Let's see . . ." Jason mused. "Why not a group program? If the Center developed and put into place a group services program, Sandra, I think the client wait list would begin to drop and our workload would become more sensible. Besides, we both know that groups work!"

"Yes, yes, yes, let's go that way. I really miss doing groups! I knew the center wasn't into groups before I came, there were lots of other good things going on here, but what a lack. But is this a doable thing?"

"Well, I don't know," confessed Jason. "But maybe the first thing is that we have come to something that we feel strongly about. That's got to be a good step. Now, let's see how it could be done—how can we get a group program going at the center?"

Jason and Sandra Develop a Strategy. "Obviously, we can't do this alone," offered Sandra, as she thought aloud. "Don't we need to get all the staff involved?"

"Nah, that would take forever," warned Jason. "We need to get going with this. Time's not on the side of the center here!"

"But look, Jason, wait a minute," rushed in Sandra. "I am brand new here, just about, and you haven't been here too much longer. I'm afraid it would be suicidal for us to try to go it alone!"

Of course, Jason thought to himself, I've had to watch out for this before—rushing ahead, being too headstrong. Thanks to Sandra for catching me.

"You're right, Sandra. I just got going too fast. Thanks for bringing me back to earth. Let's back up to your point. How should we get others involved?"

"Well," mused Sandra, "it just so happens that we are in charge of arranging the next clinical staffing—set for a week from tomorrow, isn't it? What if we used that meeting to surface our idea?"

"What a great idea! And how about this one—we form the staff into a task group. Then we could get them to discuss the idea and also to experience the group format. What do you think of that, Sandra?"

"Great, I think—but how would we announce this to everyone? There is always some kind of agenda put out before."

"I don't know, just do it!" Jason was getting somewhat impatient, but he caught himself and thought further. "Let's see, let's call it what it is, at least sort of—something like 'Groups as an Approach to Client Service.' "

So Jason and Sandra developed the memo and sent it to staff:

EASTLAND HUMAN SERVICES CENTER
INTERNAL MEMO

TO: Clinical Staff
FR: Dr. Freed and Dr. Arnold
RE: Clinical Staffing Meeting: May 4, 10:00-11:00, Room 15
DATE: April 26

Our next clinical staffing will focus on "Group Services as an Approach to Client Care." It will vary somewhat from our usual format, as no specific case will be considered. Rather, we would like to conduct a group discussion of the topic. Attached is a reading we think you might find interesting and that might serve to guide our discussion: "The Role of Group Services in Mental Health Centers."

We look forward to our discussion. See you there.

Mary Tomlinson, the clinical director, was sorting through her mail and other communications the next morning and found the memo from Jason and Sandra. She raised her eyebrow while reading, aware that the plan proposed was not the usual way of doing business at the center. As well, though plans for clinical staffings did not need to go through her for her stamp of approval, most often they did, at least informally. But then again, she was no "control freak," and what harm could come of it?

She moved on to her 9:00 appointment, setting the memo aside on her desk.

Some other staff were not so charitable. Bill Symington, who had been a psychologist on the staff since the center's start, some 26 years ago, plainly did not like either what Jason and Sandra planned to do or how they had announced this to everyone else. Over coffee with three other close colleagues, Gloria Robbins, Judy Denson, and Jerome Brown, he let them know his feelings. They too were unhappy about it.

No conversations occurred between other staff and Jason and Sandra about the memo. The leaders approached the clinical staffing meeting on May 4 with high hopes and great excitement.

Performing

Room 15 was a "catch-all" gathering and meeting space for the staff. This is where staff meetings, celebrations (such as holiday lunches), and any "schmoozing" before and after client sessions all occurred. The room held no more than 20 people and was sparsely but nicely furnished. In its center was a long, rectangular conference meeting table, surrounded by comfortable chairs. Little space beyond that was available. An interior room, it was ungraced by windows or live plants. However, a tall artificial ficus tree stood in the far left corner, and four beautiful prints decorated the walls, one scene for each season of the year. The one item of obvious extravagance was the stately grandfather clock located catty-corner to the ficus.

Jason had presented at three previous clinical staffings, the last one with Sandra about a couples case they were conducting. No problem—therapists get used to these kind of meetings, and sometimes they even can be very helpful. Yet he was curiously anxious about this one, probably because clinical staffings usually went by the same format of case presentation followed by analysis and recommendations. The format of this one would be different.

Jason and Sandra had agreed to meet at 9:50 on May 4, just to get oriented before the meeting. As can happen in a busy agency, however, each was late, arriving just before 10:00, so that they had no time for getting themselves together. As they rushed into the room, others were beginning to gather as well.

Staff members came in, each taking his or her customary location around the table. This seems to be a rule in staff meetings, where everyone has his or her own territory staked out. Not having worked this out in advance, Jason and Sandra quickly decided to sit next to each other at the head of the table, given that this was "their show." Mary Tomlinson sat next to Sandra in the third seat at the head. Another eight staff members were seated around the sides of the table, with Bill and Gloria, Judy and Jerome seated across from each other. A few minutes of chitchat went by about the forecasted rain, last night's ball game, and their big caseloads. At 10:10, Mary, the clinical director, began, as usual.

"Good to see all of you this morning. Betty called in sick today, as some of you already know, so we will be one short. But let's get started. We all got a memo from Jason and Sandra about their plan for today's meeting. My first reaction," she offered with her nice warm smile, "was that this seems quite different but no doubt will be interesting. Let's see where we go with this," she concluded, nodding at Jason and Sandra to begin.

Jason began, noticing with some surprise that his voice was seeming to waver. "Thanks, Mary. Yes, in our memo Sandra and I tried to let you know that our meeting today will be a little different than usual. Instead of examining a clinical case, we thought we would just facilitate a group discussion about the center and let the center be our 'case.' "

Bill Symington's eyebrows arched, and he began tapping his pen on the table. Some others moved in their chairs.

Jason quickly continued but wondered if this was coming out just right. He was aware that his anxiety was rising.

"Well, by that we don't mean that anything is wrong with the center, just to take a look at it and how we might be able to progress. As Sandra and I have talked about it, we thought that some focus on using groups in the center would be really worth exploring. That's why we attached the article, which we hope you had a chance to read."

Stares all around the table. Silence that you could cut with a knife. Squirming. Looking down, just like in school when the teacher asks a question and you study your shoelaces.

Jason, forever the intrepid one, persisted. "We all know about how our workload has been getting heavier, and the client wait list. Maybe, Sandra and I thought, some of this is due to our use of individual therapy as a main approach. You know, we can see only so many clients that way. On the other hand, groups would allow us to see more people with fewer staff. I mean, it would be more economical—"

"And groups are effective, too," inserted Sandra, looking perhaps overly enthusiastic, as eyes turned toward her. "Lots of research cited in the article pointed that out."

Jason felt that his heart was ready to burst out of his mouth. For a staff that was nearly always responsive during these meetings, this reaction was very strange. No eye contact, no responses, except he noticed that Bill and Jerome, seated next to each other, seemed busy exchanging notes and that Jerome and Judy caught each other's eyes.

But pressing on, Jason said, "Yes, lots of research, and there are many models of how groups can be used in an agency like ours, as the article described." And in an effort to appear casual and to try to more clearly open the discussion to others, he concluded, "Well, enough of our rambling. Can we get started with our discussion? How about this—what are your thoughts about using groups at Eastland?"

Silence, again, at least in words. Loud speaking without words. Jason saw shuffling in seats, clearing of throats, eyes looking at the ceiling or the floor or darting about. A few people seemed buried in the article. The sound of the grandfather clock tick-tocking away was all too noticeable.

Sandra jumped in, not knowing what else to do. "Maybe we could begin by taking a look at the article. What struck you about it? What did you think about the Seligman study on the effectiveness of groups?"

More tick-tocks; now about 30 minutes had passed. Then, straining against the silence, Mary, feeling her duties as clinical director, broke through.

"Gosh, this seems strange. I don't know, does anyone have any thoughts?"

Bill Symington, the senior staff member, who always showed his affect by the color of his face, blurted out, red-faced, "Well, I don't know what's going on here, Mary. This whole thing just seems absurd!"

Jason was angered. Why is Bill talking to Mary? It's our idea, no matter how bad it might be! And where does Bill get off with being so upset?

All eyes turned to Mary, the clinical director, whom Bill had addressed. She wanted to support her young staff members, Jason and Sandra, and what they were trying to do here. Bill could be cantankerous, but his intuition was more frequently right than not, as she knew from years of working together. Searching for some compromise, Mary responded.

"Bill, I'm not sure where this might be going either. I am interested in it going somewhere, though. We've got about a half-hour left, so let's move ahead by talking about that article."

"I didn't like it, Mary," replied Judy Denson quickly. "Groups might be okay in many settings, but they are not a panacea. The author clearly had a point of view, and I don't like to be brainwashed."

"Me either," said Jerome. "Plus, his assumptions were faulty. How can groups be used if clients don't want them, as we know?"

A conversation had begun, and it was centered on the article, just as Mary had asked, with staff speaking directly to Mary. This negative critiquing of the article continued for nearly 20 minutes.

Jason and Sandra found themselves at a loss during that time. Though they heard what was happening, each was caught up in his or her own worries. Jason noticed his gurgling stomach and realized that the flow of the discussion was all wrong, but he did not know what to do about it. Sandra experienced an impulse to interrupt the discussion and say something like "Wait a minute here, let's talk about our center," but she kept returning to a recurring tape that was playing in her mind: "Hold on, you are too new here, you have nothing to say."

Now the meeting was just about over, with less than 5 minutes remaining. Jason, Sandra, and Mary all were unsure of what to do. Bill spoke.

"Well, we're just about out of here on this one. Time's up. No disrespect intended," he said, looking at Jason and Sandra, and then, to Mary, "We didn't get anywhere today. I think we'd best return to our clinical staff format and deal with some of the tough cases we have before us."

Mary attempted closure: "Well, yes, we are out of time, and I know we all have other appointments." Seeking still to support the efforts of Jason and Sandra but agreeing with Bill, she added, "Getting us to talk about issues like this is good, I think, but maybe we should find a different way to do it." Turning to Jason and Sandra, Mary suggested, "Let's get together to brainstorm some, okay?"

And with that, the meeting was over. As everyone scurried out of the meeting on their way to next appointments, Mary caught Jason and Sandra, smiled warmly, and said, "Four o'clock today, okay?"

Processing

Jason was glad for the upcoming meeting but wished he and Sandra could talk first. No chance for that today, with the outcomes evaluation team that he was on meeting during the lunch hour. There was so much undone. There were so many loose ends. As he walked out of his office to meet his 11:00 client, he wondered, what had gone wrong?

They gathered at 4:00 in Mary's attractive office. He had always felt so safe and secure here, everything was so—he didn't know just what—*cozy* was the best word he could find. He and Sandra sat next to each other on the sofa while Mary sat across from them, behind a small table whose top contained a stunning collection of precious paperweights.

"So," gently began Mary, "we had a very unusual meeting today. Have you two had a chance to discuss what happened?"

"No," both said at once. Jason added, "We've been tied up with other things; wish we could have." Sandra nodded in agreement.

"Okay, well, let's spend some time now, shall we?" offered Mary. "I have until about 5:15; then I have to get downtown to the board. Are your schedules all right with this?"

"Yes, let's do that, cause it was a mess and I don't really know why," confessed Jason. "Usually things go so well—" Again Sandra nodded, looking anxious.

"I'm not a group expert, by any means," said Mary. "But the meeting felt awfully uncomfortable, that I do know. Let's start with that; how did it feel to you two?"

Sandra burst forth, "Terrible! I felt so unable, so unprepared." Jason noticed that her eyes were glistening, with tears welling.

"I felt like a complete incompetent," he disclosed. "Just not sure from the start about what to do, and that was very surprising. It felt like a total failure, for us and for getting all of us to consider groups!" He felt very vulnerable.

"Yes, I see, and I'm not too surprised about your reactions. You are both so good at what you do, so committed, and not having something go right is just something you're not used to." She let that sink in and then asked, "Well, what do you think led to this happening today?"

Jason expected this question to be coming. Good supervisors do not usually provide the answers, but they ask the right questions, allowing the supervisees to discover new ideas and to learn from their experience.

"We didn't start out right, not together," suggested Sandra. "We planned on getting to Room 15 ahead of time to get oriented, but we didn't do it because of running over, and then I never felt on top of the meeting at all. That's the first thought that comes to me."

"And you, Jason?" asked Mary.

"Yeah, that's very true, I felt unprepared—and I always like to be prepared. Somehow I'm thinking we may have rushed this, not developed the whole idea along the way."

Mary had helped Jason and Sandra put their finger on a real problem, that of failing to plan and to prepare not only themselves but also other staff. Although they recognized that certain aspects of the meeting itself could have been improved, including Mary's own intervention of focusing on the article rather than on how people were feeling, the stage was set for failure earlier on, during planning. Jason and Sandra began to see how they had developed their own solution to a problem they had defined without involving any other staff, or the clinical director, in the process. Jason certainly recognized this problem of rushing ahead as a recurring one for him. When the typical clinical meeting format was altered, it was done so in advance, but again without seeking anyone else's input, even Mary's. In retrospect, this all looked so clear, Jason concluded. They had jumped the gun quite badly, leaving their colleagues out of the process and then expecting them to fully participate just the same. Then, when the meeting actually happened, no one was willing to follow along, and the very best leadership skills could not have saved the day. They had lost the meeting before the welcome by not attending adequately to planning.

ANALYSIS

Follow the Best Practice Guidelines

When developing a group or a group program, leaders must attend to a variety of needs and imperatives. The planning phase of group leadership assumes heightened importance. In the case just presented, the leaders gave insufficient attention to planning, and the results became quickly and painfully obvious during the clinical staff meeting.

Leaders must be aware of best practices and seek to include them in their work. Jason and Sandra diagnosed an agency problem (low staff morale and compromised client service), determined a solution (group program), and tried to begin work on it (clinical staff meeting), all before enlisting administrative and colleague support. Although having good intentions and perhaps even an accurate perspective on what was wrong and what was needed, they violated the planning guideline "Be Aware of Professional Context" (see Chapter 1). As a result, colleagues were unwilling to become involved, demonstrating their resistance during the task group meeting through negative nonverbal behavior, avoidance, and confrontation.

If Jason and Sandra had been responsive to this planning guideline, they might have first discussed with the clinical director, Mary, their impressions of what was not working in the center and their tentative idea for addressing it. Securing administrative support is a necessary early step. If Mary agreed with their analysis, Jason and Sandra might have then discussed with her how to address it. A collaborative approach in a system, such as a mental health center, nearly always works better than one taken independently. Mary might have taken a more active role herself in authorizing processes for enlisting broad staff input as they worked on the problem, developed a potential solution, and engaged in program development. As a result, a task group meeting such as that conducted through clinical staffing might have occurred, but with obvious administrative support. This would represent a significant change, as other staff would understand that the idea about developing a group program was not the agenda of two junior staff members only.

Considering their approach to the clinical staff meeting itself, the leaders failed to determine their mutual roles and functions. Though they had set aside 10 minutes just before the meeting to get oriented, this did not occur. Even if it had, 10 minutes is not enough time to accomplish this activity. Coleaders need to set aside sufficient time, protected from intrusions or cancellation, to carefully plan their sessions or meetings and to identify their mutual responsibilities. Doing this would have greatly assisted Jason and Sandra during the meeting.

Utilize Group Work Competencies

As was pointed out in the discussion of processing above, in this case example the best skills would not have corrected the errors resulting from planning. However, better delivery of certain core competencies might have helped.

Better planning of their mutual roles and responsibilities might have assisted Jason and Sandra to avoid excessive talking at the beginning, especially that done by Jason. As well, adequate planning of the meeting might have produced better balance between the involvement of the two leaders and clarified their role with that of Mary, the clinical director.

Jason seemed to be observing and identifying member and group process events during the meeting, as he observed uncomfortable silences, unproductive nonverbal behavior, the passing of notes, and other such negative member participation. However, he found himself unable to respond effectively. In fact, both leaders became caught up in internal dialogues centered on their anxieties, taking away their ability to remain focused on the members and the group.

As a consequence, the leaders did not address member behavior, their own thoughts and feelings, or group process. They colluded with the members to avoid these important processes by continuing to talk about content, a faulty direction that was exacerbated by the later involvement of Mary. Instead, the leaders might have intervened at the group process level, by questioning what the silences meant or by wondering what members were thinking and feeling.

Through fuller attention to planning, the task group meeting would have gotten off to a much better start, providing the opportunity for good performing skills to propel the meeting forward. As it was, the helpful intervention of Mary at the end of the meeting ("finding another way"), followed by the processing session among Mary, Jason, and Sandra, might still have saved the day, allowing for future attempts to occur. In group work, all is usually not lost by a few mistakes if leaders can adjust accordingly.

QUESTIONS FOR REFLECTION AND DISCUSSION

1. A personality characteristic of Jason that proved to be a problem was his tendency to act impulsively. It is important for group leaders to understand themselves and be self-aware. How about yourself? What are your strengths and weaknesses as they may relate to group leadership? To task group leadership specifically? Reflect on these questions, and jot down your responses. If possible, discuss these with a partner.

2. What are the advantages and disadvantages of groups? Can a group program be expected to contribute to improved staff morale, as well as client service?

3. If you were in Jason's shoes and decided to seek to introduce a group program in the Eastland Human Services Center, how would you have gone about it?

4. Jason and Sandra were taken aback when staff did not respond actively and positively during the meeting. How do you imagine you would have felt in that situation? What, if anything, would you have done differently? Why?

5. What have you learned from Jason's predicament? How might you apply this learning in your future group work?

CHAPTER 3

The Task Group Leader Should Not Deliver Group Counseling

BACKGROUND

Dr. Virginia Hetter had come to the University Counseling Center just about a year before as a new staff counselor. A recent graduate from an outstanding doctoral program in another state, she had joined a mostly veteran staff composed of four full-time and three to five part-time staff, the latter depending on contractual arrangements with the counseling and psychology departments that changed each semester. Virginia was selected from a pool of applicants for a host of reasons, including her excellent academic record, strong group counseling skills, and specialization in chemical dependency counseling. In addition, interviewers were uniformly impressed with her clearly strong motivation, as she had put it, "to make a difference."

Making a difference had become an organizing theme for her life. Although Virginia was aware that it was traceable to her family history, she did not have a firm grasp on just how strongly connected it was.

The known facts were that no one in her family had ever been able to even dream of college. Her parents were both bright enough and easily could have attended the local college. But there had been no models of this in their families growing up, no encouragement, and certainly no money; for as long as they could remember, they had been consumed by trying to make ends meet. David and Sarah, her older siblings, had made it through high school, but just barely, and for different reasons. David, especially, had had a rough time. He had found school a real trial, and he was more often than not in some sort of trouble. By his sophomore year, the family had become aware of David's marijuana usage and binge drinking, which explained a lot of his problems. But, like many parents, they had no idea of what to do about this except to ride it out and to scold, yell, and pray. By some stroke of good fortune, final grades had come, and David had made it; he would graduate, just barely, and on time with his class.

The elation they had all felt about what must have been a miracle was quickly and irrevocably shattered on graduation night by the dead-of-the-night knock on the door, and the cop's "I'm sorry—I have to inform you that. . . ." David had been killed instantly in a car crash, and the toxicology report issued later showed he had been driving under the influence of alcohol, registering a blood alcohol level of .20, twice the legal limit in the state. This was a blow from which the family, and certainly Virginia, had never recovered.

Her sister, Sarah, had found a boyfriend early, not too long after David's death, and her attention had turned there prematurely. Along with working around 20 hours a week as a waitress at various restaurants in town, she just did not have the energy or time to devote to school. Although probably gifted, Sarah had managed just narrowly passing grades, finally getting married halfway through her senior year—not as dramatic a tragedy as David's, but nonetheless a loss.

Perhaps as a reaction to all of this, Virginia had very early set herself on a radically different course. By third grade, she had declared that she wanted to go to college, very unusual for a child of that age. Where this came from was a mystery to everyone, but she was determined. Spotting a raw talent that needed support and direction, her fourth-grade teacher had taken Virginia under her wing, letting her know, in so many indirect ways, "You can do it!" By sixth grade, Virginia had adopted the words of Abraham Lincoln that she had discovered in a history lesson: "I will study and get ready and someday my chance will come." By seventh grade, she was writing to colleges around the country requesting their catalogues. It was amusing to her that more often than not application forms also were enclosed.

The words of Lincoln continued to provide a blueprint of sorts for her as she moved through life, especially through school at all levels. Now, with the dissertation done and graduation freshly behind her, after 9 years of college and graduate school, Virginia was finally through! It really didn't seem possible to her that she was at this point in her life, and she was happy that her family seemed proud of her and not at all resentful.

She was determined to prepare and to make a difference in the lives of others through counseling focused on substance abuse. By so doing, she reasoned, she would be able to make a real contribution to others, atone for her brother's grisly and untimely loss of life, and maybe salvage some of her family's history. All of this, of course, was a big burden to be carrying, and Virginia was not fully aware of its size or weight. But, like Lincoln, she had studied and gotten ready, and now her time had come.

As would any other new staff member, Virginia had spent her first year at the center getting oriented and finding her place. Beyond that, she had begun to make a mark by asking for and getting assigned most of the substance abuse cases, the number of which was growing. She saw most of these students individually at first and then began to offer groups for them. Groups were fairly new to the center, with individual work predominating.

But there was no problem in either offering these groups or filling them. Other staff were eager to refer from their caseloads, fully recognizing that Virginia was the "staff expert." Assignments from intake also seemed to work well. So the last third of her first year found Virginia running three "substance abuse counseling groups" a week, in addition to other responsibilities. She was very pleased and felt that she was making a difference.

About 5 weeks into the fall semester of her second year at the center, during Homecoming weekend, a tragedy occurred that stunned the campus and surrounding community. Following an off-campus Homecoming dance, on the drive back to campus, a car carrying six university students ran off the well-lit, straight road and crashed into a huge maple tree. It was determined that the three couples had been killed instantly. Later toxicology tests revealed that the driver and all but one of the passengers had been legally drunk at the time of the accident. According to an eyewitness account in the local newspaper, the car had been seen speeding erratically a few minutes before the crash.

One of the first calls came to the on-call telephone crisis service operated by the Counseling Center. The counselor on call was asked if two staff could go immediately to the accident scene, where some distraught students had begun gathering. The next few days involved counselors' visiting student residences and conducting crisis intervention debriefing sessions with affected students. Referrals were made to individual counseling sessions at the center, and groups were established to continue debriefing and lend support.

Besides therapeutic responses to need, discussions sprung up both on campus and in the community to openly address the prevalence of substance abuse. Many parents called the university president demanding that the university take some "action to stop this kind of slaughter from happening" and wondering, "What kind of university are you running, anyway?" Editorials in the city newspaper called for "swift and sure steps to assure a safe learning experience for all students." The faculty senate passed a resolution requiring that "Student Services at once institute substance abuse programs for all students." And the student body president, observing the obvious place of alcohol at many faculty center functions, exclaimed, "Yes, students must be taken to task regarding alcohol abuse, but so must our sometimes all too righteous faculty and administrators!"

Two weeks following the tragic accident, the university president announced the creation of a University Task Force on Campus Substance Abuse Prevention. Task force membership represented all major sectors of the university. And the chair of the task force was Dr. Virginia Hetter.

ACTION

Planning

Rumors about the formation of a task force had been circulating around the campus for a few days. Bill Loud, the Counseling Center director, was being consulted about its membership. He realized that there should be representation from the center on the task force, and Vice President Thompson was encouraging him to pick someone to chair it.

He couldn't argue with Thompson's point. The center staff had the needed expertise, and besides, the task force was a place where the center should be involved for political reasons. But chairing this thing? This would be a very big deal, with lots of pressures and tensions around it, and very much in the public eye. Who could do it?

He immediately thought of Virginia Hetter, dismissed the thought due to her youth and inexperience, but kept coming back to her. She was the obvious choice due to her work in substance abuse counseling. In a short time, she had established a reputation as a great therapist who really could work well with substance abusers, especially in groups. As her supervisor, he had been able to view her work closely, and he was very impressed. But he seriously questioned if she was ready for such a sensitive and responsible position. "Hell," he muttered to himself, "*I* wouldn't want to take this one on!"

After mulling it over and over, Bill decided to sound out Virginia about the task force. "Who knows," he thought, "maybe she'll want to do it."

When he first approached Virginia about the task force, she was supportive of the plan. "Yes," she agreed wholeheartedly, "putting together a task force is a great idea. The president is doing just the right thing, I think."

"It does make good sense," added Bill. "Thompson wants the center to be involved," he added, edging further.

"Oh, yes, definitely," Virginia enthusiastically agreed.

"Yeah, he wants someone from here to chair the task force. Now that's a big job. . . ."

Virginia arched her eyebrows and blew out her breath, just a little, on that one.

"Virginia," Bill continued, deciding to plow ahead, "I am thinking of you for that position, you know, chair. I don't know, in most ways you would be great for this, but it really is a huge, public job." He trailed off, allowing her to think and reply.

Virginia's first reaction was one of terror. Then she fairly shrieked, "I couldn't do that! I mean, I haven't been here long enough, I don't know the people, no, no, it just wouldn't work!"

Although Bill was surprised by the intensity of her reaction, he completely understood her point. "It's a lot to ask, and I can appreciate your feelings about it. We can pass, or maybe you might want to be a member?"

After her outburst, Virginia suddenly felt calmer, more in control. "What an opportunity," she thought. "If I really want to help things to change, here I can put my money where my mouth is."

"I'm sorry, Bill," she said. "Can we go back? I think I might be interested in the chair role. Can we talk more about it?"

After further exploration and asking for a day to think about it, Virginia agreed to become the task force chair.

Three days after accepting the role of chair, Virginia and task force members all received an appointment letter from the president:

OFFICE OF THE PRESIDENT
201 GRIMSLEY HALL
INTERNAL MEMO

TO: Dr. Virginia Hetter, Counseling Center Chair, University Task Force
        on Campus Substance Abuse Prevention
      Dr. Fred Jenkins, Psychology Dept.
      Dr. Nancy Ewing, English Dept.
      Dr. Mildred Jones, Student Health
      Dr. Billy Boynton, Student Services
      Dr. William Eakins, Vice Provost
      Captain Ernie Doyle, Campus Police
      Ms. Annette Sams, Greek Advisor
      Mr. Samuel Tripecka, Alumni Association
      Dr. Terence Floyd, Student Activities
      Mr. Jorge Hernandez, Student Body President
      Mr. Ted Abramson, Interfraternity Council
      Ms. Susan Meade, Panhellenic Council
      Ms. Jennifer Watkins, Neighborhood Council
FR: Franklin Johnson, President
RE: The Task Force
DATE: November 14

I want to take this opportunity to thank all of you for agreeing to serve on this critically important task force. Perhaps never in our history has the university directly experienced such a tragedy as that of the auto accident that took the lives of six of our fine students over last Homecoming. While we all grieve for their loss, I have determined that we also must take what steps we can to prevent any such catastrophes from occurring in the future.

Please provide the results of your deliberations to my office, including specific recommendations, by April 1. We have assigned the task force meeting space in the President's Conference Room. I am asking George Seidman, my assistant, to check with you about day and time. You may begin at your earliest convenience. If you need any resources to help conduct your task, contact George at 548-4123.

Thank you once again.

Cc: Vice Presidents
      Deans

A rush of panic took hold of Virginia as she quickly read the memo from the president. She felt lightheaded and flushed and had to immediately sit down.

She reread the memo, this time more slowly, trying to calm herself. "Have I gotten into something I shouldn't have?" she asked herself, followed by "Now what do I do?"

She decided to review the membership. She began by counting the names: 13 members, a very large number for a task group. She realized that she had met only two of the members before. Fred Jenkins from the psychology department was a good guy; in fact, he worked part time at the center every other year. And she had met Terence Floyd, the director of student activities, when she had presented at orientation. He seemed very gregarious and probably got along well with students. The others were all unknown quantities. Continuing by category, she counted eight men and five women; two minority members (Billy Boynton and Jorge Hernandez); and representatives from the faculty, administration, students, police, staff, and community.

"Hmm," she mused. "The prez has put together a pretty diverse group. Wonder if any of them know each other and if they're all interested? Well, I'll wait until I'm called for more on this." Checking her watch, she saw it was time for her 10:00, and off she went.

Later that afternoon, the call came from George Seidman. After going over open days and times for the President's Conference Room (which Virginia had never set foot in) and comparing them with her availability, they picked two possibilities. George would use these times to get the best fit with the other members and would get back to her as soon as possible. The next day, she got an e-mail from George Seidman: "Virginia: We got it! First meeting set for next Tuesday, 9:00. All but Hernandez can be there then; all are on for the time otherwise. Good luck! George."

So the task force was set to meet in 4 days. Mixed feelings of excitement and apprehension took hold of Virginia as she began to think about the first meeting.

She realized she had no experience in leading this kind of group. She had been in task groups countless times, as most people have. Staff meetings certainly counted, as did training meetings and committees of all kinds. These she knew about. And for the most part, she had found these meetings to be uninspiring and too often boring and without point.

The more she thought about it, the more she began to reclaim her confidence, for she had led many other kinds of groups very successfully. All of them were personal change groups, such as counseling, therapy, and psychoeducation groups. She especially loved counseling groups, had been well trained in graduate school to lead them, and felt very comfortable leading them. No doubt, she thought, she could apply her good group leadership skills to this task force too.

Performing

At 8:45 a.m. Tuesday morning, Virginia made her way across campus to the Administration Building. It was a pretty walk on a cold yet sunny day, taking no more than 10 minutes, and meandering alongside a series of gardens recently put in by the local horticultural society. But today Virginia noticed none of this as her mind was occupied totally by the upcoming first meeting of the task force.

Butterflies flew wildly in her stomach as she made her way into the building and up the landing, around the corner (to the right? No, to the left), and into the President's Conference Room.

She faced a huge, exquisitely buffed wooden conference table, around which were placed the most comfortable yet elegant chairs she had ever seen. She imagined the table could easily hold 20 people around its rectangular surface. Four pitchers of ice water, each circled by glasses, were located strategically every few feet, and in front of each chair on the table was placed a small notepad and pen, each embossed with the university seal. The walls were covered almost completely by gigantic paintings of very formal-looking, austere men in full pose. As they ended with a rendering of President Johnson, and as this was, after all, the President's Conference Room, she assumed these were of all the university presidents over the years.

As she was thinking about the room setup, in bustled George Seidman, President Johnson's assistant, interrupting her train of thought.

"Well, you must be Dr. Hetter," he said smilingly. She nodded. "It's nice to meet you in person," he said. "I'm George Seidman, and if there is anything I can help with, just let me know."

"Thank you, George," responded Virginia. "Can't think of anything right now, but we'll see." George smiled again, and hustled out, looking very much like a man on a mission.

Footsteps were sounding in the outer corridor, and Virginia thought, "Well, here we go."

The task force members began entering the Conference Room. Of course, she knew no one except for Fred Jenkins, who was not there yet, and Billy Boynton, who had just come in.

"Well, hi, Dr. Hetter," Billy said jovially. "Really good to see you again, but too bad under these awful circumstances."

"Yes, Billy, but—" she leaned over to him—"Please call me Virginia. There is far and away too much formality in this room already, if you ask me!"

He laughed. "Okay, sure. You know, I've been here many times before and I *never* get used to it!"

People came in and took seats around the huge table, in two cases leaving chairs between them. There was hardly any talking. She counted noses and got 11. She already knew that Jorge Hernandez, the student body president, could not be present today, and she saw that Fred still was not there yet.

"Let's see," Virginia said to everyone as she looked at her watch and then around the table at all of them. "It's about 9:05, and I think we are one short for today's meeting. Can we wait just a bit for him to come."

Just as she finished, in walked Fred Jenkins, apologizing for being late. "Damn traffic on 57," he complained. "Semi jackknifed, spilling its beans all over. Anyway, I'm here." As he made his way to an empty chair, he turned to Virginia and said, "Hi, Virginia, it's good to see you."

Virginia nodded at Fred, smiled, took a deep breath, and began to address the task force members.

"Well, here we are, and I guess we are now to be known as the University Task Force on Campus Substance Abuse Prevention. I am Virginia Hetter, from the Counseling Center, and I agreed to chair our group. We are here because of the terrible tragedy involving the death of six students over Homecoming. So it's not a happy occasion at all, but perhaps we can do some good through our meetings. Let's hope so, anyway. Maybe the first thing we could do, to get us started, is to briefly introduce ourselves: you know, name, your role at the university, anything about why you are here today, maybe. Could we begin with you, Fred?"

And so they were off and running. Introductions were proceeding well, if somewhat more somberly than they might otherwise occur due to the seriousness of the situation they were confronting.

They were almost around the table when they got to Susan Meade at around 9:35. Susan represented the Panhellenic Council, the organization of sororities at the university. She said that the three women who were killed in the car crash were all sorority members. She went on to reveal that two of them were from Susan's own sorority. She looked away from the others and tears began to well up and trickle down both cheeks. Struggling to maintain her composure, she said, "And one of them, Tiffany Tigge, was my roommate last year—we were best friends. Not only that, but, you know what? I almost was in that car with my boyfriend, but we got in the next car by mistake."

The group went silent as a tomb. It seemed as if no one knew what to do. Even Virginia. Maybe especially Virginia. Suddenly, given Susan's disclosure, this group felt like a counseling group, not a task group. She wasn't clear about how to best respond, and, not having had much experience in leading task groups, she had assumed that this kind of involvement was just not part of them, anyway.

Not knowing what to do, she reached for an intervention she was comfortable with in counseling groups: She focused on Susan and said to her, "You really are feeling pain right now, Susan. I feel really sad for you, for your loss. It must be so hard to bear—"

With that, Susan forgot she was in a room with strangers at a big, important university task force meeting. Here she was with someone who was listening and responding to her needs. Why, she suddenly wondered, had she not taken time for herself earlier than now? And why now, of all times?

"Oh, it is," she cried. "It's been so hard, I miss Tiffany so, and it's mixed up with thoughts that this could have been me."

More discussion continued at this therapeutic level, largely between Virginia and Susan, with occasional support given by Annette Sams, the Greek advisor. Ted Abramson, from the Interfraternity Council (an organization representing all campus fraternities), weighed in around 10:00. He said he had been at the Homecoming dance and was one of the students who had gathered at the accident scene. He had tried, he said, to help others to keep calm, but it was very hard. He had known all the students killed and still was shaken by the experience.

Now Virginia was becoming more aware of the task force as a whole. She had lost sight of it for several minutes, focusing on the raw emotions of Susan and now of Ted. Ten o'clock had come and gone, but because the ending time had not been discussed yet, members were unsure of what to do. Virginia had not noticed that Nancy and Terence had excused themselves a few minutes earlier, leaving a written note that they had other meetings to attend. It was now 10:15, and others were beginning to shuffle their papers, getting ready to leave.

Virginia decided she had better try to put Susan and Ted on hold and talk to the whole group. She said, "Maybe we had best stop for today and regroup next time. Would next Tuesday at 9:00 be okay?"

They all nodded while slipping out of the room quite hurriedly.

Virginia continued to work with Susan and Ted, and Annette remained as well. By 11:00, both Susan and Ted were doing better but were embarrassed. Virginia explained to them how to obtain an appointment at the Counseling Center, after they expressed real interest. In fact, she decided to walk with them to the center right then to obtain appointments.

Afterward, though, when the dust had settled some, Virginia quickly thought back to the task force meeting and became alarmed. What had happened? What had she done? How had things gotten so out of hand? Had she made some big mistakes? Would this task force be able to continue?

She wasn't sure of these answers, but she did remember that they had not gotten around the group to complete introductions. They had not discussed an agenda or goals for their meeting. They had not determined how frequently and for how long they would meet. She was not able to mention that one of their numbers, Jorge Hernandez, would be joining them next time, that he could not make it today. They had not begun to coalesce as a group; in fact, they may have been blown apart. Much was left undone and, indeed, she felt that the Task Force was now in a state of disarray, if not destroyed. She was frightened by that possibility.

She found herself "going through the motions" all afternoon, being unable to dislodge the events of the morning's meeting from center stage. Late in the afternoon, after her last client of the day, Virginia finally had some free time. After weighing the pros and cons, she decided she needed to talk about the situation. She called Bill to see if he was in, admitting to him quickly, "Bill, I really need some help with this task force. Our meeting this morning was a disaster!"

"Please come down right now," he urged, in his typically reassuring voice.

She had never been more thankful.

Processing

Although he was the director of the center and was necessarily preoccupied with a myriad of administrative tasks, Bill had not lost either his love for or his skill in clinical work. And he was a wonderfully supportive supervisor! Virginia always felt very comfortable coming to Bill with questions and concerns about her work.

Typically, they met weekly for 1 hour to discuss work in general and examine any cases that were especially challenging Virginia. They also had handled the occasional crisis on a "must-see" basis. This was one of those times, and Virginia knew this was the biggest crisis of her career.

Bill's door was open, and he was seated away from his desk, ready to talk with her. That's another thing she liked about Bill: He was very focused, and when he talked with you, he was always very present.

Virginia rushed in, having no need to hide her feelings and appear supercompetent when she felt incredibly vulnerable. She plopped down in the chair she had sat in so many times before, usually in better circumstances, caught Bill's eyes, exhaled with a whoosh, and spilled out, "Help! I think I blew it this morning!"

Meanwhile, Bill had gotten some unsolicited feedback about the meeting just before Virginia called. Bill Eakins, vice provost and a task force member, had called out of concern to say that the meeting had been, in his words, "quite tense and very unusual." He seemed to think that the task force was off to a very unsettling start and even wondered if it should be reconstituted. He'd give it another try next week, though, because maybe things would improve. As he signed off, he hastened to say that Virginia had done a great job in "comforting" some upset students.

Bill had hung up being uncertain about what to do about the phone call from Eakins, but he thought it would be wise to talk with Virginia soon about how things had gone. Her call soon after the vice provost's was most propitious.

"Wow, I can see you are really upset about it," said Bill. "Can you tell me what happened?"

"Well, I'm just so concerned that the whole thing might be ruined. I mean, I got so caught up with the grief of one of the student members that. . . ."

Bill interrupted her. "Whoa, come on, just slow down for a minute," he gently suggested. "Let's take this one step at a time. Try to describe for me as accurately as you can the events as they occurred. Let's use our usual supervision style. Then we'll look at what these things might mean and their implications. How's that?"

"Good," Virginia said, and meant it. She appreciated the orderliness of the process, which was one they were both familiar with.

So she began with her anxiety on entering the President's Conference Room and went from there. She described the physical arrangement of the room, how people sat, and the lateness of the start and then high-lighted the "go-round," with its focus on Susan and her response to Susan's issues.

Bill listened intently, painting a mental picture of the situation. He asked only one question: "What were the others doing during this time?"

This question cut to the core of the problem—Virginia could sense that immediately.

"Ouch," she exclaimed almost viscerally. "You've hit it right on the head. I've got to admit," she confessed with shame, "I wasn't even looking at them. I was so caught up with the student's grief."

Bill observed, "Yeah, I was getting the sense that you might have been conducting some individual therapy within the group and that maybe you had forgotten the group at the same time. What do you think?"

Virginia could only agree. "Yes, no question about it. And I wasn't even aware of it. You know, that kind of mistake would never happen in a counseling group of mine."

"Can we consider what all this might mean, Virginia? And where to go?" With this question, Bill was moving the supervision to a deeper level, beginning to examine what could explain these events and what they might mean.

Virginia was very eager for this to happen, and said so. She needed to better understand what occurred and to see if she might be able to pick up the pieces.

He then asked a follow-up: "Virginia, what is the purpose of the task force, its agenda, and how are you all going to work on those things?"

As she responded, Virginia realized more fully that none of these questions had been addressed in the meeting. "I'm embarrassed to say that I just don't know, and we didn't get at any of these things today." Again, she felt near defeat—the task force was probably doomed.

"Okay, hang in there, let's keep going, shall we?" said Bill, with encouragement. She nodded.

"Virginia, reflect on this: What would help to explain why you focused on the student's emotional experience—in a task group—and missed giving attention to goals, methods, and all the rest?"

"I really am not sure, I sure got off center. But you know, I just felt so overwhelmingly sad for her, almost as if. . . ."

Here she suddenly stopped, with a sharp intake of breath, as an insight rushed to the surface.

She went on slowly, formulating her words as her insight developed more clearly. "I think it's tied to David. David was my brother, Bill, and he also was killed in a car crash. He was out celebrating his graduation from high school. No one thought he would ever make it, but he did. He was driving home, and it turns out he was drunk. He hit a tree. It was—it still is—awful!"

She cried, letting loose years of untapped grief of her own. Bill waited patiently and supportively, beginning to understand how Virginia had been trapped by her own unresolved grief.

After awhile, Virginia went on. "It's funny, isn't it," she said, looking at Bill, "that David's death is so strongly with me today." Leaping ahead, she added, "And Bill, while the student's grief was real and there was a need there, it was *my* grief that led me there, kept me there, didn't allow me to pay attention to the group!" She was angry at herself for this.

Yet becoming aware of this issue and tying it to the task force experience had a clearing effect on Virginia. They talked about this for some time and then moved to next steps.

"You know, Bill, finally realizing this about myself is all well and good—I really mean that—but I've got to figure out what to do about the task force. Like, is it salvageable? If so, how? What can I do?"

"What ideas do you have?" Bill asked, hoping to draw them from her now that she had gained greater self-awareness.

"I feel much more optimistic now than an hour ago when we began," said Virginia. "All may not be lost. Let's see, back to when the student became so emotional. Instead of reinforcing that and getting caught up in it myself, I might have suggested to her that she and I could talk about her feelings right after the meeting, or something like that, and then I could have tried to continue moving the group on to finishing the go-round and getting into goals. What do you think?"

"Sounds like a critically important and very different response," replied Bill. "And I think very appropriate for your task force at that point. Offering to follow up right away with the student, hopefully, wouldn't have turned her off but would have let her know you were concerned. Good!"

Feeling encouraged, Virginia continued. "Then back to the present— what would you think of my writing a short memo to the task force members before next meeting to remind them of the meeting and to give them a suggested agenda of what we will do then. Something like mission, goals, time line, and so on. I feel a real need to catch up with everyone, to quickly try to get back on track with them, and then to follow through during the meeting. What do you think of that idea?"

"I like it. Good idea," said Bill also remembering his earlier phone call from Eakins and his concerns. "It will help to reestablish the fact that the task force has some kind of product to generate and it is not a therapy group—despite what the first meeting might have looked like."

"Okay, Bill, don't rub it in," joked Virginia, who was now feeling much more in control and very relieved.

All at once she was looking forward to the next meeting with greater clarity about how to proceed—and with a deeper knowledge of herself.

ANALYSIS

Follow the Best Practice Guidelines

The case demonstrated the importance of group leaders' being self-aware, a key "best practices" tenet, so that they keep their personal issues from affecting the group experience. Virginia's unresolved grief resulting from her brother's untimely alcohol-induced fatal car crash years before led to her inappropriate focus during the first task force meeting.

Further, the case example illustrated the importance of group leaders' matching their interventions to the group type being provided. Virginia was essentially conducting group counseling, focused on grief expression and resolution, within the first session of a task group. The different intervention that she proposed later to Bill would have served to redirect attention from deep personal sharing to more of a task focus without brushing off Susan's genuine and important concerns.

Utilize Group Work Competencies

The case also shows how essential task group leader skill competencies were not used. Through allowing herself to attend to the grief of Susan and later of Ted, Virginia failed to focus and maintain attention on task and work issues, obtain goal clarity, mobilize energies toward a common goal, implement group decision making, manage conflict that was emerging, blend a task focus with appropriate attention to human relations factors, and be sensitive to larger organizational and political dynamics surrounding the task force.

It is not at all uncommon that counselors who lead task groups get caught in precisely the same kind of issue that Virginia faced. After all, of all forms of group work, task groups generally are the most "foreign" to many counselors. The focus of task groups on performance and production runs counter to what comes naturally for counselors: paying attention to human interaction. Unless they are careful, counselors can fall into the "feelings trap," where every problem or issue is addressed by attending to affect first or only. Of course, in task groups, this approach surely is a trap because the main issue in them is getting work done. The task group leader must keep this need as the primary agenda, using human relations as an important supportive means toward helping group members reach their task goals.

Virginia got off track by reversing this order of priority, in part because the content of Susan's revelation touched off her own unresolved personal issues. In addition, as pointed out earlier, it may just be less complex and more comfortable for many counselors (serving as task group leaders) to deal with feelings being expressed than to focus simultaneously on both feelings and task.

The emphasis placed by Virginia on feelings occurred during the first meeting of the task force, when most groups are at a most fragile state of development. Therefore, the very existence of the task force was threatened.

Virginia's processing with Bill and what came out of it may help her to resuscitate the task force. Implementing these ideas may reestablish the task force, allowing members to give proper attention to determining goals, method of working, and other necessary agenda items. Moreover, Virginia's insight about her unresolved grief may allow her to perform more effectively in the future, rather than to be victimized by her own experience.

QUESTIONS FOR REFLECTION AND DISCUSSION

1. Some people think mistakenly that leading task groups is easy. Considering Virginia's case with the task force, identify sources of challenge that she had to face. For each one, imagine how you might have behaved. What similarities and differences emerge?

2. All group work leadership has the potential of "pushing the buttons" of the leader. This happened to Virginia in ways she had not even envisioned. What are your personal "buttons" that you need to be aware of as you lead groups?

3. Though sharing much with other types of group work, task group work involves some unique competencies. What are they? How do they differ from, say, group counseling competencies? How did Virginia "get her wires crossed"?

4. Being able to plan and to process one's group leadership with a trusted colleague is critically important, as Virginia's work with Bill illustrated. What is involved in making these relationships helpful and productive? How will you (or do you now) address the matter of colleague support in your group leadership? What format would be helpful?

5. Managing content and process is vital in task group work. What happened in Virginia's case? What is your capacity to do this balancing act well?

PART III

Psychoeducation Groups

Garpp, the Psychoeducation
Group Leader

Psychoeducation groups include the presentation of content material focused on the issues being faced by the group members and consistent with the purpose of the group. Garpp, the psychoeducation group leader, is conducting a commonly occurring group of this kind, addressing stress management.

Cartoons by J. C. Conyne. Used with permission.

However, Garpp makes a mistake that is committed by many psychoeducation group leaders. That is, he lectures to the members, droning on and on, failing to provide the members with opportunities to interact with him, the material, or each other. This approach blocks the use of interactive processes and prevents members from getting involved and learning from one another. As in the task group example, Garpp errs by not harnessing the power of group process. A good psychoeducation group leader can appropriately blend both content and process.

Cartoons by J. C. Conyne. Used with permission.

CHAPTER 4

Missing the Driving Force

BACKGROUND

As the first session of her psychoeducation group approached, Donna Trammel was becoming more and more anxious. This was the first psychoeducation group she had led.

Donna had been a social studies teacher for 9 years, starting right out of college. She loved teaching social studies, taking great pride in her lectures and in directing historical role plays in class. She had a great ability to make history come to life. She also loved working with students through her role as advisor to the History Club. However, teaching had lost a lot of its luster over the years. She was beginning to feel that she was doing the "same old thing" over and over. Lacks of adequate classroom supplies and equipment were additional irritants. And discipline problems were getting to her. Increasingly, she was feeling more like a warden, or maybe a cop, instead of a teacher.

After 5 years of teaching, Donna decided it was time to make a career change but to remain in the schools. As much as she was losing interest in teaching, she couldn't imagine working outside the school. It was all she knew. And she had always felt that school is where the action is. She still wanted to be part of the action—maybe, even, to be able to change some of that action somehow.

Therefore, she applied for and was accepted in the school counseling program of the nearby university, focusing on the secondary school level. After 4 years of working and going to school, Donna graduated with a master's degree. School counseling seemed to be just the right fit for her, as it would allow her to work directly with students, as well as with teachers and parents.

During graduate school, Donna's training in group work was probably insufficient. She realized this because when the program sought accreditation, its group work training was cited as needing improvement. Further, she was not especially interested in group work and did not usually feel comfortable in group settings. She found groups to be too ambiguous. She thought that the leader should be much more in control of what goes on in a group instead of using the "laissez-faire" (her term) leadership style that she had learned in graduate school.

During her training, Donna had learned about a type of group work called psychoeducation, which fascinated her. She was attracted to it because the leader seemed to be much more in control than in other kinds of groups. She also found the use of structured exercises to be very sensible. However, Donna had not been able to acquire any experience with psychoeducation groups during her graduate training. Her one supervised leadership experience had been in group counseling, and it had not been a particularly joyful time for her. Again, the lack of leader control that seemed to her to be a part of counseling groups rubbed her the wrong way.

Yet Donna knew that using groups within the school was a desirable and certainly necessary approach. She was committed to seeing as many of her advisees as possible, and she realized that a group format could provide many assets that individual meetings could not. Besides, the counseling department was expected to deliver groups from time to time.

Interestingly, the kind of groups that tended to be offered in the school were psychoeducation groups. The director of counseling, Tom Stephens, was a firm believer in their utility and asked that each counselor offer two of these groups per term. Donna met with Tom weekly to discuss her work, and during each of the meetings they had given some attention to psychoeducation groups. With his supervision, Donna felt confident in being able to offer these groups effectively.

One of the suggestions that Tom made early in their discussion of a psychoeducation group was for Donna to create a detailed group plan. He pointed her to several examples of group plans in the department's file that she could look at in developing her own plan. Every winter term, at least one psychoeducation group was offered on stress management. Tom thought that this topic would be a good one for Donna to consider.

Donna went to the file and selected five samples of plans, three of them on the topic of stress management. She saw that their formats were all generally alike, including in some way:

- General scope of the group: Type of group (task, psychoeducational, counseling, psychotherapy).

- Population: For whom the group is offered.

- Philosophy: Line of reasoning on which the group is premised (e.g., by teaching stress management skills, the members will be able to be more effective students).

- Conceptual framework: Theoretical and research knowledge that will be used to guide the group (e.g., cognitive-behavioral, humanistic, primary prevention).

- Nature of group: Remedial, developmental, or preventive.

- Content of group: Information and skills to be covered in the group.

- Goal(s): Concrete, behavioral statements about what members can expect to learn.

- Format of group: How many sessions, length of sessions, exercises and structured experiences, use of adjunct structures, such as video or homework.

- Group development: Group progression model that is used to create the group plan (e.g., formation, control, work, termination).

- Process of group sessions: Generally following a cognitive-behavioral approach, beginning with presentation of material for the day, demonstration, member practice, feedback, additional member practice, and processing of the session.

- Leader role: Leader is facilitator, not expert.

- Process of each session: Goal(s), method, roles, resources, time, processing. (Conyne, Wilson, & Ward, 1997)

To Donna, developing a plan including the elements above seemed both important to do and relieving at the same time. As a teacher, she had, after all, developed lesson plans and curriculum guides for years. She imagined that transferring her planning skills from the teaching domain to that of the group leader should be easily accomplished. As well, going into a group with a plan in hand served to remove a tremendous amount of anxiety that she was developing about leading a group. It took away so much of the ambiguity and provided a sequenced

approach that would serve to guide her group leading. So she went about
the task of planning her stress management group.

ACTION

Planning

Donna took each step of the planning format in order, starting with
the general scope of the group and ending with the format for each 2-hour
session of the nine-session group. This work yielded a 12-page document
that was quite thorough. The department typically did not screen students
for these types of groups, and there had been no screening before this
group. Students had signed up for the group on the sheet that Donna had
distributed following three talks she had made in classrooms, and teachers also had referred students. On the basis of these recruiting and
referring approaches, Donna expected six students for the group. Having
completed the task of designing the group, she felt confident and optimistic.

However, the one area that still gave her some concern was that of
leader role. It seemed that there was so much packed into the group
overall and within each session. She wasn't at all sure how she could get
all the information disseminated and the skill building accomplished and
attend to process as well. It seemed that she might have to behave less
like a facilitator and more like an expert, but she wasn't at all sure of
that. The whole area of leadership seemed quite confusing to her.

In her next supervision session with Tom, Donna showed him her plan
and asked for some feedback.

"Here it is," she said. "I feel pretty good about it. Those other plans
were very helpful to me."

Tom scanned the plan. He was very used to looking at them. He could
see that she had done a fine job of addressing the points and organizing
the material. He suggested that she might reduce some of the goals to
make the plan more feasible. They talked about where this reduction
could occur.

"Okay, this is looking more doable now," Donna said. "But you know,
I'm still having some trouble with imagining how all this can get done,
especially when the leader needs to present so much information and do
skill training. What about attention to process?"

"That's a keen observation, Donna," said Tom. "You've hit the nail on
the head, especially with psychoeducation groups. It really amounts to

a balancing act. Leaders learn how to balance content and process through experience, I'm afraid, through trial and error. But the great thing with you is that you have already identified a potential problem area, and this might help you to be more attuned to it from the beginning. I think the best approach at this time is just to go ahead and see what happens and then figure it out later."

Although Donna thought it might have been better to spend more time on the leadership dilemma of how to balance content with process, she went along with her far more experienced supervisor.

"Okay, then, here we go. I'll be back in after the session is over."

The first 2-hour session had been thoroughly planned. At 2:00, 2 hours before the first session, Donna reviewed once again the sequence of activities she had created. First, she intended to greet everyone as they came in and spend some initial time with introductions. She knew the importance of building a sense of connection and developing a working climate of trust. She planned to orient the members to the group goals, to develop ground rules for the group, and to identify individual member goals. This session called for helping the members to understand the concept of stress and how it can be manifested. This goal would be met through a didactic presentation she had developed on stress and how it can generally affect high school students. She then would ask members to provide examples of how they experience stress, focusing on school situations involving academic or social applications. Next, she would try to develop a discussion among members about the commonalities and differences they noticed in each others' statements. Following this discussion, she planned to teach them the skill of relaxation, using the Subjective Units of Distress Scale (SUDS), giving them practice in its use during the session, and discussing how they might plan to use it during the next week. A homework assignment would be given, based on use of the SUDS relaxation training method. Finally, she planned to conclude the session with an open period of discussion, focused on members' thoughts and feelings about what happened in the session and encouraging them to reflect on what they had learned.

"Whew, this sure is a lot of material to cover," Donna said under her breath as she closed her planning book and began to ready herself psychologically and emotionally for the task ahead. She worried, "I'm still not confident about how to do all this." Her mind raced with all kinds of misgivings and wishes: "Maybe I should have a coleader, maybe I should have spent more time working this through with Tom, maybe I shouldn't even be leading groups at all!"

In this way, Donna worked herself into a state of considerably anxiety, approaching the first session on very shaky ground indeed. Yet at the same time, she had the wherewithal to exclaim to herself, in complete amazement, "Darn! Members will be anxious, too—maybe more!" But it was too late to practice relaxation now, she thought. And then she walked through the door into the group room to ready it for the group.

Donna was 15 minutes early. She wanted the group room to be set up right, with chairs in a circle, and no mess around from other groups. She also realized that this was a way for her to control her mounting anxiety.

Having set everything in order, she scurried out quickly to get a cup of coffee in the staff lounge. Energy is what she needed, and caffeine might be just the thing. She must have seemed very pressed because Judy, their caring and ever-present secretary, asked her if everything was all right and if she could help Donna get anything. Donna had not even noticed her there, really, with her thoughts being totally consumed by the upcoming group session. She lied, in as upbeat and nonchalant a voice as possible, "No, Judy, thanks. Just getting ready for group," and hoped Judy bought it.

Returning to the group room, Donna waited for the members to arrive. It was now 3:58.

Performing

The short of it is that the first session looked nothing like the plan. Everyone came, the group met, Donna led—oh, how she led—and the session ended. But there was a gap the size of the Grand Canyon between intentions and reality.

What accounted for this immense gap? Donna's biggest fear of being unable to blend content and process was realized. The session was similar to a small class where the teacher presents information in a didactic manner. It was not quite a lecture, but a series of inputs in which Donna disseminated information, defined terms, gave examples, and described procedures. When she stopped herself, on the very few occasions, to elicit member participation, she did so by asking questions, some of them very good ones ("How do you experience stress in your lives at school?") and some not so good, being closed-ended ("Does everyone understand the definition of stress?").

Donna was not all that unaware of what was happening. She remembered saying to herself, about halfway through the session, "This is really bombing! Stop talking so much!" But she could not match her self-talk with appropriate action. She kept talking, delivering important information but failing to involve the members as participants. It was as if she just could not stop, even though she thought she probably—no, make that, must—do so. She was out of control, feeling like a blithering idiot, but talking just the same, lecturing, delivering, falling back on tried-and-true classroom teaching methods of Socratic questioning, fighting to pull the session out of what she feared could be a disastrous outcome—leading heroically, struggling and working very, very hard.

Toward the end of the 2 hours, though, Donna was pleased that at least no one had walked out. "Well, it can't be all *that* bad," she told herself.

Some even looked as if they were following her, maybe benefiting from the information. She couldn't be sure, of course, because she had not followed the part of the session plan that provided an opportunity for members to discuss the session and what they had learned.

Now, checking the clock, Donna was startled to find just 10 minutes remaining, after it had seemed to her to be stretching unendingly, punishingly, for most of the session. She was aware of feeling exhausted but wanting very much to carry over whatever positive energy might exist among members to the next session.

She concluded the session by going over the homework assignment, reminding members how they were to apply "SUDS," and passing out the exercise. She said she hoped everyone had found something of value in the session, and she mustered up enough strength to indicate that she was looking forward to next week. (As she said this, she wondered how genuine it had sounded because in fact she wasn't very sure of it.) She smiled, looked around the room at each member, and said in as encouraging a tone as possible, "See you next week!"

Members left the group and walked from the room showing varying degrees of energy. Some had smiled back at her and nodded at her invitation to return for the next session. These students, maybe numbering three, seemed involved. The other three appeared impassive, nonexpressive, as they left, much as they had looked throughout the session.

Donna, herself, crashed. She sat numbly in her chair for what seemed to be a very long time, unable to summon up the necessary energy to move. She felt psychologically and emotionally clobbered. At that point, she didn't know why—she couldn't put her finger on its causes, and she was not at all ready to even try. She felt, deep down, that she desperately needed a respite, some sort of sanctuary for awhile where she could lick her wounds. Then, she hoped, she would be ready to meet with Tom to get some help.

After her time alone, which must have been no longer than 15 minutes, she pulled herself up and made her way out of the group room. She realized that she needed some fresh air and some distance from that place. She would write notes and reflect later.

Once home in her apartment where she lived alone, Donna settled in, cooked up the leftover stew she had made, and called her best friend, Margo. She just needed to chat about anything but work and see what was on Margo's mind these days—they hadn't talked in more than a week or so. Talking with Margo almost always did a world of good for Donna. Margo matched Donna's typically serious demeanor with a cheerfulness that sometimes seemed otherworldly to Donna. But maybe that's why they had been best friends ever since they had met in graduate school.

Donna drew strength from their discussion, which, although about "nothing," really seemed to be about "everything." It took her away from the group for a short time, and that was just the medicine she needed. After hanging up, she felt ready to meet with Tom to take a good look at that group.

"Oh, my," she sighed to herself with anxious anticipation, as she prepared for bed.

She awoke early the next morning after a fitful night's sleep. She had tossed and turned most of the night, with images of the group dominating her attention and refusing to loosen their hold. She finally dropped off to sleep after what seemed like hours and dreamed, once again, a familiar nightmare.

In this dream, a shipwreck was occurring, maybe something like the Titanic disaster. All on board were facing drowning, and the big ship was going down, down into the deep ocean. Chaos prevailed, with no one in charge and all about to perish unless something could be done—unless someone could do something very heroic to save them. As all looked lost, she awakened from this dream, as before, with a start and breathless, her heart pounding wildly.

Donna had experienced this nightmare on two other occasions over the last 4 years or so. It was nearly always the same, including her sudden awakening. The first times, although they were scary, she had quickly moved on with her day, giving little thought to what the dream might mean or to why it had occurred. Teaching and graduate school combined had left little time for such a luxury. Now, though, with the dream appearing as it had immediately on the heels of the upsetting group session, she felt some connection emerging for the first time, but it was still not in clear focus.

Sharply defined was the need for her to meet as soon as possible with Tom to go over the group session. As she prepared for work, she decided to stop by his office at 8:00, before they had settled into the pace of their respective days, to see if she could get some time.

Processing

Tom always could be counted on to be at work by 7:30 every day. He was a great guy and also a workaholic, one who seemed to give his "all" to the Counseling Department. One of his better qualities was that he would somehow make time for staff when they needed him, even though his own appointment calendar typically was crammed. A corollary weakness, not uncommon for people like Tom, was that he often spread himself way too thin. He was usually on the go, needing to be someplace else fast. This tendency sometimes led to compacted meetings or to rushing through meetings. But his many assets far outweighed this problem, and Donna had found Tom to be very supportive and helpful during the last year—and there whenever she needed him to be.

There was no exception this morning. There was Tom's car parked in its customary spot. She went to the department office, where Judy greeted her warmly and, probably remembering yesterday afternoon, asked again if she were all right. After assuring Judy that she was fine, Donna asked if Tom was available for a few minutes.

Judy replied, "Yes, Mr. Stephens is in—of course, what do you expect?" and laughed while shrugging her shoulders. "You know, sometimes I think he lives here! Let me see if I can free him up for you, Donna," she said, going into Tom's office.

Judy returned quickly, telling Donna to go straight back— Mr. Stephens would of course see her right now. As Donna walked quickly back to his office, she felt a bit like a bad student being summoned to meet the principal.

Tom dispelled her trepidation immediately by his friendliness. "Donna, good to see you this morning," he bubbled very cheerfully. "Come in, come in, have a seat. What's up?" Tom always liked to get right down to business quickly, probably due to his fast-paced style.

"Tom, I need to talk with you about my first group session yesterday," she began, not sure just where to go with it.

"Okay, let's do it," said Tom. He glanced at the wall clock and said, "I could spend, oh, maybe 20 to 25 minutes now, and if that isn't enough, we can look to another time. How's that?"

"That's fine. I think this might take a little while."

"Well, let's see what we have," offered Tom. "As I recall, you are beginning a stress group and we looked over the plan, which was a good one. How did it go?"

Finding her humor from somewhere, Donna began. "Well, everyone stayed," she replied with a sheepish grin.

"That's a good sign for sure," Tom played along, as they edged into their processing. "Now what did they do when they were there?" he asked.

"You know, I don't think it's so much what *they* did or did not do, but what *I* was doing, and feeling."

"Okay, good. Let's talk about you in the group, can we, Donna? Tell me more about what you were doing and feeling there."

"This hurts to talk about, Tom, I have to tell you that. I found myself talking, talking, talking. It was so weird. Maybe there was just so much planned that to get it all done, it really was necessary that I presented so much information."

To this, Tom asked, "I wonder if you could have stopped at any point in there to let members get in?"

"I could have, should have, Tom, but somehow that was the last thing I was able to remember then. I had the strange sensation of standing off from myself, looking at what was going on, and knowing that it was just not going well—that I was filling the air and not letting them get in—but being totally unable to change it. Boy, was that frustrating—and I felt like a failure. And I still feel right now like a failure!" With that last revelation, she cried softly.

Tom let a silence build for a moment as he remembered their last session. Donna had raised the issue of content and process, along with her uncertainty about how to balance them appropriately in the psycho-education group. She had seemed afraid that she might tend toward relying on content, or at least that bringing attention to process matters might pose a big difficulty. He realized that he could have been more helpful to her at that point, thereby lessening the problem she had experienced.

"Donna, you are hurting about this experience, even now, it's clear," he said gently. He paused, while she nodded in agreement, feeling understood. He went on, "But there is no need for blame here. If there is any blame at all, maybe I should accept it for not being more responsive to your concerns last time we talked about balancing content and process. Am I remembering that correctly?"

Again, she nodded, recalling that she had wanted to spend more time on this issue then. Maybe that would have been helpful.

"Yeah, I did want to look into that more back then. It might have helped, Tom, but working this out through experience—as you suggested then—still is needed. Except the experience hurts!"

"Maybe more than it should," he added. "I know I could have been more helpful when you asked, and for that I apologize. But maybe we can move on now. What's done is done. Are you wanting to?" he checked with Donna.

"Oh, yes, if we still have time," she said.

With that, Tom stepped out, called to Judy, and asked her to postpone his next appointment by 30 minutes.

"All clear," he announced. "Let's continue."

While Tom was briefly out of the room, Donna flashed on her nightmare of last night. What was that all about? Was it in any way connected to her experience in yesterday's group?

"Okay, let's see," she began, trying to get back to the group. "I keep wondering why I kept going, explaining, reexplaining. Is this the teacher in me? But I can't lay it on that. No. . . ."

Tom broke in. "Can you remember how you were feeling during those moments? Anything about self-talk at those points?"

With that, Donna gazed away from Tom slightly and to her left, settling for a moment blankly on the familiar painting, deep in thought. "Yes," she started. "Yes, I was feeling some desperation about things not going well in the group, out of control almost and, and . . . something more, that maybe I was responsible and needed to take charge. Yeah, that's it, I felt like I needed to kind of save the group!"

Having said this, she was startled by the obvious connection of her experience in the group and her recurring nightmare. It all very suddenly made perfect sense to her. The group was like the sinking boat, and she had stepped in as the heroine-savior, struggling vainly to right its wrong, to keep it afloat by leading through talking and explaining content, leaving absolutely no room at all for group process and the involvement of members.

She looked at Tom with a new alertness and excitement. "I've just realized something I think is very important," Donna said. "I think I was trying all I could do, which was mostly talking and explaining content, in order to keep the group going and to prevent it from falling apart. Tom, I think I was trying to save the group, as stupid as that sounds now! And I worked so hard at it, took all of this on myself, as the leader, that I trapped myself into allowing no room for members to participate or for discussing what was happening in the group."

"Gosh, that really seems like a significant insight, Donna. You have put this together very quickly. How does it seem to you?" asked Tom.

"Yes, this does seem important, as if I've been able here to identify deeper reasons for why I just kept filling the air. And I'm thinking that with this awareness now, I'm freed up from running the show, doing everything."

Tom agreed, offering an extension: "Yes, and maybe you can find ways to make room for members to take part more fully. Instead of running the show, as you say, you might be able to share the show with them more."

"Oh, I like that idea very much. Now the question is, how do I do that? And how can I begin doing it this very next session?"

"I have a couple of suggestions for you to consider, Donna, if you like."

"Please, let me hear them," said Donna.

"Okay, let's see. You might think of introducing to the group members next time that the first session was more of an orientation to the group, kind of getting started. And in that, you took a much more active and prominent role than you will in the next sessions. You could suggest that gradually more and more opportunity will be given to them to get involved and talk with each other and about the group. After all, you could point out, the group is for them to benefit from—it is, in a very real sense, their group. And you might follow this up, depending on how things go, by asking them how that sounds and what they have thought so far about the group. How does that kind of approach sound to you, Donna?"

"This is good, very good. I like the way you are suggesting to help maybe build a bridge between the first and next sessions and the idea that the group is ours together. The part about asking them for their reactions to the first session is kind of scary, though. I mean, I thought it was disastrous!" Donna said.

"Good. Well, maybe asking them is scary and you will decide to stay away from it. But you really have no idea about how they did feel about the session, right? You didn't give them much of a chance to get that in, I guess."

Donna knew this was true, and also that she would need to begin including opportunities for members to process their group and how it was going.

"Of course, you are right, Tom. I'll work on myself. It's more me than anything else, and this morning I feel like you have helped me make some real strides. Tom, I think this is going to work!"

ANALYSIS

Follow the Best Practice Guidelines

Donna was not ready to lead this group. Her training and experience with groups was limited, and she had had no previous experience with psychoeducation groups specifically. Her competence as a group leader was undeveloped, and she possessed a fragile confidence as she approached the first session. In addition, she was haunted by personal issues about which she was unaware. These personal issues, revolving around taking control, turned out to directly affect her application of group leadership, as she was unable to put brakes on her relentless need both to run the group and to single-handedly keep it from failing.

On the positive side, Donna did have a conceptual idea of how to lead groups and what might be required especially in leading a psychoeducation group—the challenge of appropriately balancing content and process. Her overall group plan and its session-by-session components were based on tested models, had been reviewed with her experienced supervisor, and had been modified where needed.

Utilize Group Work Competencies

Problems arose during the first group session when the plan was not implemented. Donna found herself being victimized by a combination of her relative inexperience with group leadership and with psychoeducation groups particularly. This led to her inability to harness the "driving force" of group work and to focus, instead, on content delivery nearly exclusively.

Her approach to Group Session 2, emerging from the deep processing of her meeting with Tom, seems positioned for greater member involvement. As she is able to more fully include the "driving force" of group process and member reflection into her group, its chances for success will improve dramatically. And, as an important side benefit, she will not have to suffer and struggle along the way.

Skillful processing of the first group session with her supervisor enabled Donna to become aware of both her personal issues and how she was not harnessing the group's driving force. Tom helped Donna to integrate her group leadership behaviors, oriented around presenting information, with her feelings and thoughts about those behaviors. His probing also helped Donna to make a connection between how she had behaved during the group session and the theme of a recurring nightmare, even though he did not know this. This deep processing was a powerful insight for Donna. It assisted her to understand a motivating psychological need to take charge in situations that seemed somehow threatening and its relationship to her approach to group leadership. From this processing session, Donna emerged with not only insight but also some clarity about how to behave differently in the ensuing group sessions.

But an earlier session with her supervisor, geared toward the planning phase of group work leadership, pointed to how insufficient processing of important material can contribute to ineffective group leader functioning. Had Tom been willing to explore Donna's concerns about group leadership, especially how to manage content and process appropriately in the upcoming psychoeducation group, her very difficult first group session might have been more positive. Simply asking her to be sure to consider the relative weight she was assigning to content compared to process might have been enough at that point to help her preparation. But his advice to learn through trial and error, probably born out of his busy schedule, missed what Donna needed at that point. She needed to process this concern and to learn from it as she prepared for the first session. As it was, she went into the session with excessive anxiety, minimal confidence, limited experience, and a leadership model that was influenced strongly by personal forces of which she was unaware.

QUESTIONS FOR REFLECTION AND DISCUSSION

1. Sometimes counselors get called on to deliver services for which they may not have been adequately prepared. To some extent, this was part of Donna's problem. How was this so? What are the competencies needed to conduct psychoeducation groups? Where do you stand in relation to them? What do you need to do to achieve competency?

2. Consider the "driving force" in group work. What does this term mean? How did Donna fail initially to capture it? How do you imagine you would have approached this situation?

3. Donna seemed to be experiencing noticeable performance anxiety before her first group session. How do you usually feel before your first session? Other sessions? During sessions?

4. Have you ever felt that a group session you were involved with was "bombing?" As a member? As a leader? What was happening? What went through your mind? How did it feel? What could you have done to help the group to maintain itself? In Donna's case, what would you have done?

5. This case shows how significant good processing is to assist in improving a group. What did Donna do with Tom, her supervisor, that promoted positive movement? What did Tom do? How do you behave in supervision? What can you (and/or your supervisor) do to improve your capacity to process such dilemmas?

CHAPTER 5

Lacking a Plan

BACKGROUND

It had just worked out that way, for no particular reason and with no precedent. Long-time staff members of the agency and close work colleagues, Sherry Swanson and Mike Beacham had each taken late summer breaks, returning to work at the University Career Center 2 weeks before the beginning of the fall semester. Among other things, this meant that they found themselves deep in the hole of work buildup, while facing the onslaught of the new academic year.

There was no procedural problem with their having taken that time to be away. Dr. Akeem had approved each of their requests, although somewhat reluctantly due to possible timing problems. Generally, staff were expected to be back 1 month before the start of fall semester to ensure that everything was up and ready to go for all that the new year inevitably brings, both anticipated and unexpected.

The uniqueness of their requests, however, led to their approval. Mike's father, who lived alone back in Georgia, had become seriously ill, requiring Mike to fly back to help take care of his needs. And Sherry had received an invitation to present at the prestigious International Round Table for Career Counselors, held in middle August this past year in Sydney, Australia.

Sherry and Mike returned to the staff in differing states of readiness, nearly polar opposites. Sherry's experience at the conference and in Australia had been a highlight of her life. Her paper on "The Psychology of Career Indecision" was received well, and the overall conference milieu had been very professionally stimulating. She had especially enjoyed meeting other professionals from around the world. Moreover, as this trip was her very first outside the United States, it was personally momentous. Its length nearly did her in, but the 3 days she took to scout around Sydney were supremely satisfying. She returned invigorated.

Mike's experience was radically different. Lung cancer is an unrelenting, vicious killer. His father had entered the hospital already with a Level 4 advanced case, much to Mike's surprise and anguish. The last few days before his father died were painful ones, not allowing for resolution of some long-standing issues that had stood between them for much too long. Following the funeral, Mike had returned to work feeling vanquished and depleted.

They returned to the cauldron of intense, sometimes frenetic activity that always was present in the 2 weeks preceding the start of school. Their ability to reengage reflected their respective conditions on return from their trips. For her part, Sherry jumped in with lots of energy, whipping through the work awaiting her, both old and new. Mike, as could be expected, had to push hard to get through the correspondence, phone, and e-mail messages that had accumulated; picking up with preparation tasks was a bit easier but not much, especially at first. After the first week back, though, his normal buoyancy and energy level were beginning to return, despite his feelings of sadness and remorse.

In addition to normal workload issues in the center, an unfortunate event had occurred just after Mike and Sherry had left for their respective breaks. Sam Burdsall, a staff member for 2 years, and a good one too, had been offered and had accepted a position in another university. Claiming it was an offer he just could not refuse, and lamenting the sudden timing of his departure, he was gone. Given the appropriateness of this move, those left behind tried to feel positively about Sam's leaving, but that was difficult—especially when it meant that everyone would be affected by added tasks and responsibilities until a replacement staff person could be hired. Of course, obtaining permission to hire would be the first step in the process, and this was becoming increasingly difficult now at the university. Consequently, staff were on edge and feeling burdened.

One of the needs that emerged early in the new semester was to find staff to start the career development psychoeducation group that had been on hold since the last term of summer school. This was a group normally led by Sam, but because he was no longer at the center, it needed to be picked up by other staff. Because students had been already admitted to the group and had been waiting now for about a month, it was important to get it up and running as quickly as possible.

Dr. Akeem approached Sherry first about this group. In a way, he felt she "owed" him the favor of doing this group, but he didn't put it that way to her. She had past experience leading counseling groups that he thought she could draw from, she was very knowledgeable about career development, and she usually was willing to go the extra mile. When asked, she agreed to do this, despite the extra work, in part because she felt obligated due to his approval of her trip to Australia, but more so because it was a better alternative than some other things that had to be done due to Burdsall's unexpected exit. But because she had not done this group before, she felt it was very important to have a coleader. Even though it would take up more limited resources to use coleaders, Dr. Akeem quickly agreed to her request. He asked her with whom she might want to work. She immediately thought of Mike, although she wondered if he would be up to it. She suggested Mike to Dr. Akeem.

"An excellent choice, Sherry. I know you two have worked well together in many projects, and in leading groups, too—what, counseling groups?"

Sherry nodded in agreement, smiling.

"Well, how do you feel about approaching Mike about this, Sherry?" he asked. "It's an overload, of course, and we are all trying to be respectful of Mike's grieving right now. What do you think?"

"I don't know, to be truthful, Dr. Akeem. All I can do is ask him, leave it up to him, with no pressure. It might be something he would find appealing."

"Okay, then, go ahead, Sherry. Hope he can do it."

"Oh, one last thing, Dr. Akeem. No doubt I can get this from the Group Book, but when is this group scheduled to begin?"

She was not prepared for the response.

"Ah," Akeem stammered a bit, "it needs to begin next week sometime; these students have been waiting for too long already. I'm sorry about the time pressure. But there really is no way around it."

"Well, that's a problem, Dr. Akeem. It leaves no planning time for us at all. But if that's what has to be done, then I'll do it, you know that."

"Thanks, Sherry. And good luck, again, with Mike."

"The last thing I need, Sherry, is anything more to do," was Mike's initial reaction. "I'm still having some trouble finding enough energy to do things. But I don't know, I guess this might be good for me, cause I love doing groups, and working with you would be great, as usual. When would this begin?"

"That's the real clinker, Mike. Guess what? Dr. Akeem wants this to get going next week, depending on a schedule fit with everybody."

"What? I mean, today's Thursday already," growled Mike. "This is impossible. Who are the members? How many? How long is the group? What's the plan, a psychoeducation group always is planned well. Do we have any of this?"

"I looked it up in the Group Book. Yes, we know their names, there are 10 of them. The group is for 10 weeks, 2 hours per session. But, alas, no plan of any kind." Sherry sighed.

"Damn!" cursed Mike, full of frustration. He knew what this meant. Lots of last-minute shuffling and scurrying just to get the schedules aligned and the room assigned, probably leaving no time at all to do proper planning for the group.

He said as much to Sherry, and she saw it the same way. But of course, what do good staff members do in times of need? They do it. Thinking that it was probably against his better judgment—not because of her, of course, but because of the situation they faced—Mike agreed to co-lead the group with her.

ACTION

Planning

Their fears were confirmed about planning. There turned out to be no time. Their respective work schedules were so full already that carving out planning time for this new group was not possible right away. As it was, they spent whatever time available on scheduling. First, they had to find a day and time period that matched their own schedules. This is never an easy task, but it was complicated by the lateness of trying to do it against already crammed daily planners. They were able to identify Fridays from 2:00 to 4:00 as the only possibility, a most unattractive time slot for university students, unless they tried making other changes in existing arrangements. Surprisingly, when checking the calendars submitted by students, this time seemed to fit the schedules of all but two of them. These two students seemed to understand the problem, once it was explained, and were put on the next round of sign-ups. This left eight students who remained interested in the group, despite its clearly undesirable meeting time.

Finding meeting space posed no problem. The main group room was open then, so they scheduled it. At least holding a group at an unpopular time opens up meeting room space.

Having taken care of these basics, Mike and Sherry set aside Friday breakfast and lunch for doing what they could to at least outline the upcoming group. They recognized that this amount of time was terribly short and compressed and wholly unsatisfactory. Yet they also were keenly aware that they had no alternatives. So they did what they could with what they had. Sherry remembered what seemed to be almost the mantra of one of her professors, sharing it with Mike: "Group work leaders need to be flexible." Well, then, they both agreed that they qualified!

Over a light breakfast accompanied by lots of coffee, Sherry and Mike turned their thoughts to the group. They had found nothing about the group when they looked in the files yesterday. It had been one that Sam had done routinely each semester, and only he had done it. He must have taken any materials with him, leaving nothing for modeling the group except the brief announcement that had been disseminated on fliers:

WONDERING ABOUT YOUR CAREER DIRECTION?
UNCERTAIN ABOUT WHAT TO DO WITH YOUR LIFE?
WANT TO LEARN SKILLS FOR MAKING CAREER DECISIONS?
COME TO THE UNIVERSITY CAREER CENTER
&
JOIN THE NEXT
CAREER DEVELOPMENT PSYCHOEDUCATION GROUP!
10 SESSIONS
UP TO 12 STUDENTS
FALL SEMESTER, TIME TO BE ARRANGED FOR BEST FIT
SIGN UP AT THE CENTER, AUGUST 15-22.
GROUP LEADER: DR. SAM BURDSALL
LICENSED COUNSELOR
******NO FEE******

On the basis of the flier, during breakfast they were able to decide that the group would take career choice and personal values as its context and then would teach group members career decision-making skills. It would include structured exercises each week that would be tied to brief lectures. The exercises would help members to apply concepts from the presentations. Each session might include training in a career decision-making skill. They both deemed it important that each session include processing time and opportunities for member interaction. The sessions would follow a temporal sequence that was grounded in developmental theory.

Having gotten to that point, they had to stop for appointments. Before parting, each agreed to bring to lunch any materials they could quickly get their hands on that might help in planning the group, based on the above elements.

When they met again for lunch, Mike showed Sherry a possible format for each session that they might consider using: goal(s), method(s), roles, resources needed, time allocations, processing. It was a familiar format to both of them. In turn, Sherry had brought some handouts related to career development choice theory that she thought could provide some content direction and two different training approaches to teaching career decision-making skills. At least they had found some appropriate materials for shaping the group. Optimistic, Sherry pointed out that they had made some quick progress. Mike had to agree, but added, only somewhat in jest, "Looks great! But anything would look great at this point!"

From these materials and their own thoughts about what was necessary in beginning any group, they quickly outlined the first session, which would be devoted to orientation. They hoped that in this session they would not need to become specific anyway and that they could get some planning time somehow before Session 2 to get concrete about their planning. Completing their lunch discussion, they noted that the first session began in just 1 hour! Rushing to their 1:00 appointments, they left their lunches untouched.

Performing

Mike and Sherry arrived at the group room at the stroke of 2:00, having rushed from client sessions that had spilled over a bit. They had no time to confer, as the room already had some arrivals. As they entered the room, they were both conscious of taking a deep breath and exhaling to calm themselves.

Unfortunately, the room had not been put back together by its last users. Chairs were scattered, and soda cans were on the floor. The meeting room table, which should have been collapsed, was still set up in the corner. This is where the three members were seated.

The first task for the leaders, after some brief "hellos," was to ask the members to relocate into the group area of the room and to help them place chairs in a circle. Although this activity may have helped to "break the ice," it felt awkward and imposing.

While waiting for the other five members to arrive, Mike and Sherry engaged in "small talk" with those present. In reality, they were stalling for time by trying to ease the waiting time without actually starting the session. After 3 minutes or so, two more members arrived and sat down in the circle. Mike, getting increasingly anxious about attendance, excused himself to step out of the room to see if any other members might have called the receptionist, as they were expecting eight members. But none had. As he returned to the room, a sixth member arrived on his heels. She would prove to be the last. At 2:12, Sherry checked with Mike, and they agreed to begin the first session.

Sherry started. "Welcome to our first session of your career development group. Mike and I are very glad you are here, and one of the main things we'll do today is to get to know each other a little bit and to talk some about what this group will be about. You probably were expecting Sam Burdsall as the group leader. Sam moved to another university over the summer, so Mike and I are taking his place." She tried to present that last information as matter-of-factly as possible so as not to arouse any undue anxiety among the members. And after that beginning, the leaders briefly introduced themselves, followed by member introductions.

Sherry and Mike had done this sort of activity innumerable times in groups, so this part of the first session went smoothly. Maybe this was going to go okay, after all, each of them was thinking.

After finishing the introductory go-round, Mike asked if anyone had questions at that point before they moved on to talk more about the group and their own particular interests. Latisha, a member, asked if there were going to be any more members. Sherry responded that it was possible, because three others had been expected, and that she and Mike would be checking that during the week.

This led to a discussion about meeting time. Billy, another member, complained, "Do we *have* to meet at this time? I mean, it really sucks!" A quick chorus of agreement followed. Allison, a third member, wondered, "Maybe that's why the other three people didn't come."

Ordinarily, these kinds of mild challenges would not have bothered Mike at all; in fact, they might even be expected under the circumstances.

However, this was not an ordinary time for Mike, for he was feeling stressed due to the combination of work overload and the recent death of his father. He responded to Allison and Billy in an uncharacteristically insensitive way. "This is it," he snapped. "Finding another time just will not be possible, given schedules. Let's move on, can we?"

Even a casual observer could notice the sudden change in group temperature— and in Allison especially, who hugged herself across the chest and seemed to physically recoil from Mike's frosty reply.

Sherry tried to pick up the pieces quickly. "Yes, the schedules were all so tight. Maybe now we could take another look, especially if your schedules may have changed since you filled them out; and if the others end up not coming, it might open up some more possibilities."

Mike at once knew what she was doing, and appreciated it. He realized he had been out of place and had better monitor his impatience more closely.

Sherry's intervention noticeably helped ease the tension and restore some sense of greater security in the group. Allison, too, looked more at ease. After some discussion about day and time, they decided together to hold the matter until the next session when they would know more conclusively if those absent today would actually join the group.

Latisha was still chewing on something that was bothering her. "Well, what I want to know is, just what are we going to be doing in here? I mean specifically. I was in a group over here before, and it was very unsatisfactory because no one could ever figure out what they were supposed to be doing. I left after three meetings because I had better things to do with my time. I mean, no offense, but I hope this group will be different!"

Usually, members did not get as direct in their questioning so early. Maybe they were picking up some hesitancy or uncertainty from Sherry and Mike. Or perhaps other factors were somehow responsible, such as the delay in getting the first meeting scheduled, the absent members, and the change in expected leadership. Latisha apparently had a bad experience in another group at the center, and this was motivating her to get things out very quickly. Whatever it was, Mike and Sherry were caught off guard by the question, and their own lack of clarity about plans for the group contributed strongly to their predicament. All at once, both of them fully realized that their inability to work out specifics for this group was already posing a problem. Their hope that this could wait until Session 2 was not bearing out. They also had not had a chance to discuss their mutual responsibilities for managing each session. Ambiguity was taking its toll early, and Latisha unknowingly had forced their hand.

Her question was met with an altogether too uncomfortable silence from the leaders as they found themselves staring at each other, unsure of how to respond. Each was thinking: "Who should answer? What *have* we decided to do? Should we let them know we aren't really prepared because of how the group got assigned to us? Should we get from them what their goals are? How much time is left? What to do?"

Fumbling as if in darkness, Mike tried to recover, sensing that this was a critical moment in the early life of this group.

"Latisha, that's a very appropriate question, and I'm sorry your past group experience was not a positive one. We want this one to be much better," he began, focusing on reflection and hope. He went on to address Latisha's need for structure and specifics: "We'll get to the concrete stuff in a little while, and what we will spend our time on in here is to a large degree dependent on each of your individual goals."

This did not seem to satisfy her, however. She wanted more, from them. "Okay," she said, "but what are *your* plans for the group? I mean, the two of you," as she looked at Sherry too.

The other members squirmed a little in their chairs, evidencing some discomfort with this interaction.

Sherry interjected, deciding to convey what Mike and she had discussed about the group so far. "Well, the focus of this group will be on helping you all to explore your thoughts and feelings about possible career directions and to teach you a specific set of skills to help you become good decision makers about career options. We'll spend some time practicing these skills and thinking about how to apply them. And it will be important to learn from each other too. Frankly, Latisha and everyone"—here she looked at the whole group—"we just have not taken it beyond that point right now. As Mike said, we want to hear from you about your own needs and goals and that will help us to become more specific."

Sherry ended with this, Mike nodded his head, and both of them looked closely at Latisha, who seemed to be listening very closely.

"Well, that's all right," Latisha conceded. But then pointedly added, "Just as long as we get useful here and not just lollygag around."

"Yes, we want this group to be useful to you and to everyone," said Mike. He felt that he was finally getting more with the flow of the group. "You are already helping that to happen, I think, Latisha, by urging us to become goal directed. We will work hard on doing that. How do the rest of you feel about how we are moving ahead?" he asked the other members.

After some additional interaction about the direction of the group, most of it positive at this point, the group session came to a close at 4:00. After bidding everyone goodbye until next week, Sherry and Mike caught each other's eyes and let out a sigh. "Let's talk," said Mike.

They knew instinctively what to do. Mike, who had planned a night out with his wife, called and begged off, explaining he had to meet with Sherry about their group. His wife understood, being an old hand at this kind of thing. Sherry also placed a call, to her boyfriend, asking if it would be all right for them to catch the movies the next night because she needed to talk with Mike about their new group. No problem. It's nice to have understanding partners. So, having rearranged their plans for some Friday night relaxation, something they both sorely needed, they now had some processing time. The sacrifice of true professionals! Off to Pedro's for some good Mexican food and a quiet place to talk.

Processing

"Yikes, what happened?" asked Sherry, once they were seated in a private corner, away from others in the restaurant. "This was not one of our best moments."

Mike quickly responded. "Well, I know it wasn't *mine* anyway. I was really out to lunch for most of the session, and when I jumped on Allison, well, it just was uncalled for. I apologize, and thank you for bailing us out."

"Mike, I know how you have been struggling following your dad's death and all that. I even thought maybe I shouldn't have asked you to do the group with me—"

"Thanks, Sherry, but, no, I'm really glad you did. It's the kind of thing I need to get me back in the swing of things. You know, I started to feel more connected as the session went on. I'll be okay now, I think. I'm a big boy, don't take any guilt on. The issue is, will I be of help to the group and to you? I think it's going to work out if I stay in touch with my own stuff."

"I have all the confidence in the world in you, Mike, you know that. And I love working with you in groups! But please, let me know how you're doing and if I can be of any help, okay?"

"Deal," he said. "And the feeling is entirely mutual!"

"Okay then, good," said Sherry. "Let's see, what's sticking in my craw about the session is how unprepared we were. You know, on the one hand I didn't appreciate how Latisha sort of came at us with her 'So, what are we going to do—*specifically*?' "—aping her inflection out of frustration—"but on the other hand, we literally were the emperors without clothes there."

"What?" asked Mike quizzically. "I followed the part about Latisha—you know, her voice isn't quite that harsh—but emperors without clothes?" He laughed.

"Oh, stop teasing," she chuckled. "I mean, let's face it, she was absolutely right, we weren't ready, and our plans are less ready for the next sessions. If there was one thing that was made clear today, it is that we've got to get our act together on this, and fast."

"No question about it, Sherry. It was embarrassing and unprofessional. I mean, we know why this happened, and it certainly is not our style. But that's no excuse, and we need to plan. These psycho-ed groups need much more planning than a counseling group. You know, if we were doing one of those, like we usually do, we could afford to be more open-ended and process oriented. But we're not."

"Yes, that's true. I think we'll need to plan each session, not just to satisfy members like Latisha but to ensure a sequence to the group and allow for skill training to occur adequately," suggested Sherry.

The waitress, no doubt a university student, arrived to take their orders (with the now obligatory cheerful welcome, even in a nice place like Pedro's, of "Hi, my name is Jennifer. If there is anything . . ." yada, yada, yada), so their discussion about the group stopped. After placing orders with Jennifer, Mike and Sherry returned to business.

"Yeah, okay, we've got to plan the sessions," agreed Mike. "But when in the world are we going to do that?" He asked this in exasperation, directing the question as much to himself as to Sherry.

"I don't know," she sighed. "I'm thinking we may have to look at some time like this, maybe some weekday night. I hate to, but when else?" she asked rhetorically, looking off into space. "And, what's more, once we check with students absent from this past session, we may need to actually move the session to a more desirable time. Speaking of that, does Friday afternoon for a group really 'suck'?" She giggled.

"Well, I wouldn't use that term for it exactly," Mike said. "But let's just say that it was clear there was no one in that room who was even slightly pleased at meeting then!"

"No kidding!" replied Sherry. You know, our members don't seem reticent to express their opinions about lots of things. I wonder what that's about?"

"Maybe we just have some unusually expressive people," suggested Mike. "Or some angry people. Or, I think more likely, it gets back to the kind of herky-jerky way the group was established and our own unpreparedness for it that got communicated. All of a package."

"Yup, I think you've put your finger right on it," she agreed. "It wasn't them, it was us." Then came the food. Ravenous, they took a break from processing to enjoy their huge combination dinners. Over flan and coffee they resumed their examination, feeling delightfully stuffed.

"Ah, what a great place! I could eat Pedro's Mexican food any day of the week," gushed Sherry.

"Yeah, me, too," said Mike. "But I may be too full to continue about the group."

"No way, mister! Let's work for just half an hour more, over coffee, and see if we can make some progress," urged Sherry.

In the remaining time, they addressed some of what they needed to get done, including sharing leader responsibilities, when they would plan to conduct processing sessions, and a specific outline for the second session.

"So we'll generally work it that we'll take turns presenting information and skill training within each session and both be open to calling for processing time, is that right?" checked Mike with Sherry.

"Yes, that feels comfortable to me. How do you want to begin this for next week?"

"Well—how about if I do the brief lecture and you handle the training piece? Then next week, based on how that goes, we can consider reversing it."

"That sounds fine, Mike. Now for the content. If we focus on getting across to them the career decision-making model we use at the center and train them in Step 1, gathering information, that would be a great start, don't you think?" Moving ahead, she suggested, "I'll work up a brief lecture that can go along with the handout I showed you at lunch—wow, that seems like about 2 years ago now—and then, if you could handle training around Step 1, that would work, right?"

"Good, yes, that's fine," Mike replied. "In fact, I'll develop a general training model we might then use for each step as we go. You know, explain the skill, demonstrate it, give them practice, provide feedback, give them a retrial, and then have a general group discussion where we can process all of this. How does that sound to you, Sherry?"

"Like we should always process over Mexican food! Great," she said enthusiastically.

"Okay, then the last thing for us to do now is to set aside at least a tentative time that we will plan to meet for processing and planning the group," Mike continued. "Earlier you suggested maybe some time during the week like this; well, okay, let's do it that way, cause I can't see any other time during the day, given our schedules. What works, then? Wednesday might be a good time, assuming the group remains on Fridays. How's Wednesday for you, maybe over dinner?"

"Ugh, I hate to give it up, but fine, I guess. But only if we can keep it here, at Pedro's!" And Sherry smiled.

"Okay, you're on. And I think we are much better on track now. Last thing is: Who pays?"

ANALYSIS

Follow the Best Practice Guidelines

This group was an accident waiting to happen because the coleaders had been unable to create a group plan. Careful planning and preparation are important for all types of groups.

Leaders need to understand the overall framework for the group, what will be occurring in sessions along the way, and their mutual roles and responsibilities. Members need to be informed of general group goals, leader qualifications and experience with these kinds of groups, what will be expected of the members, and generally what group sessions will involve.

For psychoeducation groups especially, planning is vital. This is so because this type of group is based on the dissemination of specific information linked with training in related skills. Further, the leaders need to set this educational and skill-based group approach within a group process orientation, such that a reasonable balance is achieved between content and process. Accomplishing these goals requires production of a clear plan of action. A motto of the scuba diver is applicable to psychoeducation group leadership: "Plan the dive and dive the plan."

For group leaders, this can be translated as "Plan the leadership and lead (via) the plan."

In this case example, Mike and Sherry failed to construct a plan, except for a most general sketch. This situation resulted through no fault of their own; as one can see, circumstances combined to thwart their intentions. But it is important to realize that their case is not unusual. Circumstances of one kind or another always seem to arise that threaten the capacity of coleaders (or a solo leader) to obtain the time to plan their group. If it isn't a death in the family or the sudden resignation of a staff member, as in the example you just read, it might be simply the normal but hectic pace of work and daily life.

Utilize Group Work Competencies

Leaders must consciously and very intentionally allocate planning time and keep to it. It must be scheduled into their calendar, just as client hours are set aside. Then they need to resist "borrowing" from that time to meet responsibilities that they or others may consider more pressing or important.

Because Sherry and Mike entered the first session unprepared, they were generally ill at ease. This sense of unpreparedness gets communicated unwittingly to members and should be avoided. Moreover, when questioned by members about what they could expect to happen within group sessions, the leaders were unable to provide details (because they had not agreed on any yet), and their explanations were imbued with inadvertent discomfort.

What prevented a collapse of this first session was the general experience of each leader and the good professional working relationship they enjoyed. Without this solid foundation, the group leadership function might have failed during the early challenges of group members.

In this example, processing was accomplished by the coleaders. Processing together is one of the very attractive advantages afforded by coleadership. It demonstrated how mistakes made in a group session can be identified through open dialogue, with plans made to correct the mistakes.

Mike and Sherry's processing meeting was conducted in a social environment that provided sufficient privacy. This is not a typical arrangement, and it is not usually recommended. However, here the leaders were careful to select a place where they could talk confidentially about general issues, thus avoiding a focus on people and process. It is safer and more desirable generally, however, to process a group session in a professional setting where confidentiality is ensured.

The entire example illustrates the important concept that groups are generally robust, resilient entities where mistakes made do not necessarily lead to the death of a group. Rather, through careful processing leading to learning and new applications, mistakes can provide avenues for growth and change.

QUESTIONS FOR REFLECTION AND DISCUSSION

1. Planning is very important for psychoeducation groups, as this case illustrates. Why is this? What sorts of elements should be included in a good group plan? What more could the leaders have done to prepare?

2. Sherry and Mike faced some daunting challenges in their group arising from their inability to develop a plan. You read how they handled this problem going into their first session. What alternatives could they have selected? How do you think leaders can decide if they may be too upset to lead a group session? How do you think you would have handled this if you were in their situation?

3. Mike entered the group in a very unsettled state due to immediate life conditions he was facing. Consider the possible effects of leading a group when you are excessively upset or disturbed. How do you manage stress in general and when you have to perform? When is enough enough? What does it mean to be a professional who can deliver quality services even while undergoing difficult personal events?

4. Sherry and Mike were coleaders of this psychoeducation group. How did they work together? What were the consequences of their coleadership? What do you think of group coleadership? What do coleaders need to do to prepare for each session—individually and together? In general, what kind of coleader would you like to be, or are you now?

5. This group was able to be resuscitated. What accounted for this change? What was attributable to the coleaders? What to the group itself? What lessons can be learned from this example?

PART IV

Counseling Groups

Cartoon by J. C. Conyne.
Used with permission.

Garpp, the Counseling Group Leader

Because group counseling is an inter-personal problem-solving method, "work-ing together" is vitally important. Working together usually means that members inter-act with one another to learn and change and that the leader(s) are also interpersonally involved in the process.

Cartoons by J. C. Conyne.
Used with permission.

Garpp, however, continues the extreme version of "leader-centeredness" that he demonstrated with the task and psychoeducation group examples cited earlier. He distorts the concept of working together to reflect a top-down, one-way model of leadership that is generally inconsistent with best practices in group work. By making the members into followers of him, Garpp diminishes the most valuable resource of group counseling: the members themselves. A good counseling group leader knows how to mobilize members to work with one another and with the leader to reach mutually determined goals.

CHAPTER 6

Surprise and Challenge in Group Leadership

BACKGROUND

Heather and Bill were now into the sixth session of a 12-session closed counseling group dealing with spirituality that they were offering under the auspices of the local Episcopal diocese. Their group practice had been expanding since they conducted their first counseling group, some 10 years ago now, in conjunction with the YMCA.

Although their reputation was such now that referrals to groups came directly to them from other therapists in the community, Bill and Heather continued on occasion to provide group counseling through contractual arrangements with other community agencies. In addition, they had developed a viable consultation and training service focused on group work applications. This aspect of their work was becoming quite popular not only among mental health agency staff in the area but also increasingly within certain sectors of the local business and industry community.

This was the first counseling group that Heather and Bill had provided through the diocese, and their initial one to focus on spirituality issues. That was not to imply that their path to spiritual interests was taken without thought and preparation. Not at all.

For the past 5 years or so, like many other counselors, they had become increasingly aware of the significant role of spirituality in many people's lives. During this period, the topic had assumed a dominant presence in the popular media, in discussions at dinner parties, and even in informal work conversations. Certainly, in their individual counseling sessions, both Heather and Bill had noticed a dramatic rise in the number of clients for whom spiritual issues and concerns were of importance. The major professional associations to which they belong all had active divisions dedicated to the place of spiritual, religious, and ethical values in counseling and psychotherapy. Maybe it was an end-of-the-millennium phenomenon that was serving to bring attention to spiritual matters more to the fore, both in everyday life and among counseling professionals. Whatever its origins, a hunger for meaning in life was being expressed within the ongoing American dialogue.

Heather and Bill had entered that dialogue. For Bill, this had been a reawakening of his upbringing in the Roman Catholic Church. From earliest memories of childhood through high school, he had been very actively involved with the rest of his family in the church. Bill had drifted away from church during his college and graduate school years, like so many other students during the 1960s. About the same time that he and Heather had begun their private practice 12 years ago, he had reinitiated his religious involvement, this time with the Episcopal Church. Bill found himself attracted to this church due to its liturgical similarity to what he was used to, but especially because of what he believed were its more liberal social and political stances. He also had felt a different quality of involvement this time, a deeper feeling embracing the sacredness of worship and how it seemed to touch his soul. This change, he surmised, was probably due as much—or more—to his own development as to major differences between the two churches.

By contrast, Heather had grown up without any prescribed religious training. In fact, her free-spirited "hippie" parents had eschewed nearly anything that was formally organized in favor of a freelancing lifestyle. Formal religious practice did not fit into such an approach. Living for several years near the Navaho and Hopi reservations in Arizona with her family, Heather had developed a genuine appreciation, and good understanding, of Native American spirituality. She had incorporated what she had learned into her life in ways about which she had been largely unaware.

Over the last few years, she had participated in two or three professional development workshops devoted to spiritual practice in mental health, each of which she had found fascinating and compelling. Though she sensed a building interest in spiritual matters, Heather could not envision joining any sectarian religious faith, finding dogma and ritual to be more roadblocks than comforts. Rather, she had chosen in the past couple of years to revive and deepen her earlier connections with Native American practices by making semiannual "pilgrimages" to the American Southwest to participate as a learner in various ceremonial functions and healing practices. She was especially fascinated by the collectivist, group nature of many of these customs.

In parallel, both Bill and Heather had become ever more interested in the connections between counseling and spirituality, especially with regard to how group counseling and spirituality might be able to interrelate. As they began to share their respective interests, Heather and Bill decided to propose the formation of an association task force to study the nexus between group counseling and spirituality. This proposal was quickly approved, and for 2 years Bill and Heather had served as task force cochairs. This activity resulted in a set of recommendations addressing the formation and delivery of spirituality groups, a document that was later published in the journal.

The invitation to co-lead a group for the diocese came through Bill's community involvement. Tom Hennigan, director of religious education at the diocese, had known of Bill's private practice in counseling through their prior involvement as Board members of Community Way. He telephoned Bill at the office, explained that he wanted to have a counseling group started for priests across the diocese, and wondered if Bill might be interested in talking about this matter over lunch. Bill was pleased to accept, reminding Reverend Hennigan that he always worked with his partner, Heather Smith-Harrelson, to co-lead groups. Hennigan showed not the least bit of hesitancy at that prospect, and they arranged a lunch date for the next Wednesday at the diocesan cafeteria.

ACTION

Planning

Heather and Bill always met on Friday afternoon from 1:00 to 3:00, rain or shine, to review the week's activities and look forward to the next week. Setting aside and maintaining this meeting time—for over 8 years now—had proven to be very useful. Both of them cherished the time spent and attributed their successful personal and professional relationship in no small measure to it.

One of the first items up for discussion this time was the Wednesday lunch meeting with Tom Hennigan. Bill had left her a note about the meeting and suggested they talk about it on Friday. That's all Heather knew, and of course Bill didn't know much more.

Bill filled in Heather on his short phone conversation with Tom. Heather immediately was excited about the prospect of doing a counseling group with seminarians. But given her lack of experience with formalized religion, she had to admit some naiveté and a little bit of discomfort.

"You know, Bill," she began, "although I'm excited about this, I haven't had any experience at all in churches and certainly none with a seminary or with seminarians. I'm not even sure I could be classified as a 'Christian,' as you well know. This leaves me more than a little bit anxious going into our meeting with Reverend Hennigan. So I guess I'm wondering if what I bring to this—or don't bring, might be more like it—makes for a good fit. I mean, maybe I shouldn't be involved."

Bill always appreciated Heather's honesty. She could be counted on to face challenges directly, not to hide from them. In that way, she countered his more natural and, he was convinced, less healthy tendency to smooth over or to avoid troubles. But sometimes she kind of went overboard with this too, he thought, and when she did this, he could become exasperated. This was not one of those times.

"Yep, good point," he replied. "It's worth considering now, before we meet with Tom. I didn't give any of this a second thought. It was automatic when he asked; I just told him that we work together with groups. I guess I was thinking more about you being a woman, working with a group of all or mostly male priests, and I wanted him to know up front that with me he also gets you. This was no problem with him, as I said in the note. But now that you raise the point about your religious orientation, I have no concerns at all. After all, you are you, and I've never known you to judge or be insensitive, and you certainly have had all kinds of experience and a keen interest in spiritual stuff. Well, I guess that's it for me, that's how I see this," Bill finished.

Heather was silent for a moment, digesting what Bill had said. He always was supportive and encouraging, and although she trusted him implicitly, sometimes she wondered if Bill might not always level with her when he had a concern. This was one of those times.

"Bill, I really appreciate your support. Is there anything, though, that you might be holding back, any reservations about my going into this with you?"

Bill paused briefly to consider Heather's question and realized that maybe there was one thing. "Well, now that you push me a little on this, maybe it would be good for you to learn a little about the Episcopal Church, like what a diocese is. I can tell you some of this, and we can also get some from Tom. Other than that, I really do not see any problem. In fact, I think doing a group there could be very interesting!"

After spending some more time discussing some of the factors characteristic of that church, Heather became more content about her potential involvement. They turned their attention to the upcoming meeting with Tom.

"Let's talk about our Wednesday lunch meeting with Tom at the diocesan cafeteria," suggested Bill. "My experience with him is that he's a great guy, very open to differences and deeply concerned about the community and the church's role in it. I think you'll like him a lot—and he, you. So getting to know each other a little would be a good idea. Then we'd better get to his notion about a group—I have no idea yet what he has in mind for us to do."

"Yeah, I'm with you, Bill," said Heather. "And we'll want to discuss with him how we usually work in our groups, what our general expectations are for members, rules that we set, our fee, et cetera."

"Right, good idea. I think because this group will draw from priests across this big diocese, it's likely that few, if any, will have any continuing relationship with one another. Some may have only briefly met. And that would be good for our group. But we'll want to check this for sure with Tom," said Bill. "In addition to getting clearer how 'religious' and 'spiritual' differ—I can never really get clear on that and I know it will be important. Yes, we'll need to talk about these, and other, things with him."

On Wednesday, Bill and Heather drove together to the Diocesan Center, a beautiful structure located on a spacious, heavily treed lot set back from the road by about a hundred yards or so. It gave the impression of being a protected place, removed from the hustle and bustle of the world, cloistered. Heather's heart raced as she entered the vaulted front doors; she felt very much out of place and somewhat undeserving of being there.

But they were greeted immediately by the Reverend Tom Hennigan. His hearty and warm welcome helped to dispel much of her self-imposed feelings of "unworthiness." Bill was right, she thought. Tom seemed very likable, possessing a quick wit and warmth that helped to make her feel at ease. After a brief tour, they settled down for some lunch in the cafeteria, at a round table in a small meeting room just off the main dining area.

Bill and Heather learned that Tom's idea for the group was to provide interested priests with an opportunity to discuss their experiences, to develop their capacity to help each other, and to work through challenges. He did not expect Heather and Bill to focus explicitly on religious content or to be expert in it in any way. He wanted them to bring their group skills to the experience. This was very relieving to Heather; she could not have hoped for anything better.

Tom had already sent out what he called "feelers" to the priests across the diocese about their interest in participating in a counseling group. He had heard from 10 (of 110) who seemed really enthusiastic.

There were eight men and two women. They ranged in age from their mid-30s through mid-60s. They were at various levels of what Tom called "spiritual awakening," but all were doing well in their work, and Tom said he could "vouch" for them all.

Bill and Heather described how their groups usually were organized. They suggested a closed group of from 10 to 15 2-hour sessions, with the format being fairly unstructured and open for member ideas and involvement. Tom suggested that he could contact the interested members to select a best day and time to meet, keeping in mind that a couple of them would travel around 100 miles to get there.

Heather and Bill asked if they could talk with each interested priest individually to be sure the group might be appropriate and beneficial for him or her. Tom gave his permission.

All seemed to be shaping up well. After discussing their fee and confirming the procedure for individual interviews, they concluded their lunch planning with smiles and handshakes all around. "I'll get back to you soon about the day and time," called Tom as Bill and Heather got into their car.

Performing

The individual interviews, most conducted in person with three by phone, were very informative and useful. Each priest seemed to be well put together psychologically and emotionally. Not all of them were as enthusiastic initially about the group as Tom was, however. Three of them decided that the traveling distance was just too great for them to manage over a 12-week period, and a fourth decided that the group might not be a good idea for him right now. This left six members, five men and one woman, all of whom seemed motivated. As well, they were largely unknown to each other—"strangers," in a sense—a generally positive condition for a counseling group.

The first five sessions of the group were fascinating. Members seemed to readily get involved, with the nature of their discussion being centered on existential matters, values, and dilemmas that they expected to face as priests. The group was moving into a work phase quite effortlessly, with the members appearing to hunger for the opportunity to discuss deeply personal matters. Thus, Bill and Heather found themselves functioning largely as facilitators of a very active network of interactions. The group was "really cooking."

But at this, the sixth, session, something had changed radically. Members refused to look at one another, and no one was willing to begin talking. An unmistakable atmosphere of mistrust and hostility had invaded the group room, catching the coleaders by nearly complete surprise: not that conflict would surface—they had been expecting it to arrive—but that the total group would seem to be participating in sudden resistance, hostility, or whatever was going on, and that the atmosphere would become so completely different from that of the previous sessions. What was going on, they wondered? What explained it? What should they do now?

This was not a silence born of boredom or that accompanying a period of reflection. Rather, it seemed as if it was topping off or tamping down pressurized forces that were gathering to erupt like a volcano. Never had the coleaders seen such a dramatic change of direction in a group.

Fearing that this group was about to "blow," because this seemed to be a total group phenomenon and not attached to one or two members alone, Heather decided to ask a group-level, open-ended question. "What is going on here?" she asked very evenly and invitingly, sounding much more in control than she felt.

"Ask *her!*" shot back George, one of the members, pointing to Agnes. Of course, pointing out Agnes was not necessary, since she was the only female group member. Pointing, though, was another sign of upsetness. "She *violated* all of us, and we all know it!"

For her part, Agnes seemed to cringe in her seat, withering under the blitzkrieg attack of George and the glares of every other member. Then she suddenly stood up and ran out of the group room in tears, leaving the rest in varying degrees of shock.

Without hesitating, Heather quickly followed Agnes out the door, leaving Bill to stay with the other members. Because the group was no longer intact with one of the members having exited, Bill explained that they would not continue working but wait to see what happened with Agnes. He asked the members to take a break there in the room, suggesting stretching, journal writing, or silent meditation. Amazingly, they all responded appropriately, with some furiously writing and others sitting silently. George alternately sat and stood.

After about 15 minutes, Agnes reentered the room with Heather. She looked more composed, although she obviously had been crying. The members returned to their respective seats. Heather looked at them all and said, "I'm sorry for having left the group, and I wonder what's been happening here. If it fits now, I think it would be good if we could begin to understand what is going on with us today without destroying what we have put together. Bill, would that work?" she asked.

"Heather and Agnes, I'm glad you're back with us. We have just been waiting, doing other things—not group. I thought we couldn't move ahead without you. And yes, I think trying to make sense of what's going on is right on the money for now." Turning to the group as a whole, Bill rephrased Heather's inquiry: "Fill us all in. What's happened, and can we come back together?"

These questions were met with shuffling and silence at first. Heather and Bill remained silent, waiting for someone to respond. They fully recognized that this was a critical moment in the group, a crisis. They had talked often before about crises in groups and understood how pivotal they could be for either growth and opportunity or decay and failure. Right now they were both holding their breath.

After about 20 long seconds (which felt like an hour), Agnes spoke up in a quiet and shaking voice. "I feel like I owe everyone an apology," she revealed. "For running out, but I guess even more for the problems I've caused."

She looked at George, who had verbally attacked her in the group earlier, as she spoke. He leaned forward toward her, returning her gaze, but not at all belligerently.

Agnes continued. "I didn't intend to violate the group's confidence at the conference on Saturday. I really didn't," she reiterated, becoming more steady as she talked.

She seemed to have garnered the attention of the whole group, and of course they all knew what she was talking about. Although Bill and Heather did not know the specifics of what had happened, it sounded as if a breach of confidentiality had occurred. But they chose to not seek details, making the judgment that doing so would divert the present energy and focus. Instead, they simply permitted the interactions to continue.

There was a pause, followed by George speaking again, but this time in a completely different tone, softer and gentler: "You know, Agnes, I'm sorry, too, for my outburst at you. I've been thinking about it these last few minutes when you were gone, and I'm mortified. Obviously, this was not how a spiritual person should behave. I'd take it back if I could, but that's impossible, I know. But I'd like to somehow start anew with you here by saying to you that I apologize and I accept your apology too."

"It pleases me to hear your regret, George," offered Jack, another member. "Because you spoke for me, too. I didn't jump on Agnes, but inside I felt a lot of anger about what she did. It's my own response to it that troubles me as much as what happened Saturday."

Bob, another member, spoke then, saying that it wasn't all resolved and settled for him. "I guess I'm just not willing to put all this away yet. Let's face it, Agnes, we all happened to be there—plus, worse, the others who are *not* in our group but who were there too—when you broke our confidentiality in that role-play situation, and I don't know if we can ever get that sense of trust back. Let's say, I don't know if *I* will be able to feel trust and safety in here again!"

The coleaders were relieved about Bob's comments, feeling certain that he was speaking for more people than just himself. Too fast a closure on this confidentiality issue would deny the importance of contrary viewpoints and would short-circuit learning and applications to their group.

Bill stepped in at this point. "Wow, you know, I don't know exactly what happened in the role play with Agnes at the conference—in fact, I didn't even know about the conference and how you all might be there—but it sure produced lots of feelings, and it sure seems significant. It sounds like a confidentiality issue, and confidentiality, as we have discussed many times, is critically important for a group. Anyway, just so you know, this caught us"—looking at Heather—"by surprise today, but we're catching up. Really, that's not so important as your venting about it, understanding it, and then seeing what can be learned and applied to our group. Anyway, that's what I'm thinking about now. Are there more feelings that need to be expressed?" Bill asked.

Heather piggybacked on his comments. "Let me just emphasize something Bill said. I want to encourage you to examine your feelings about yourselves—I'm thinking of Jack's comments as an example—and your feelings toward each other, I guess specifically with regard to Agnes. Focusing on those can be helpful in moving our group forward and trying to regenerate the trust that Bob referred to."

Coming back to Agnes, Heather asked, "How are you doing now, Agnes, having heard all this?"

"You know, Heather, I'm still hurting inside." She paused, to catch up with her thoughts and match them to her feelings. "Hurting more for what

I did, not for what anyone did to me." Addressing George, she said, "You were awfully harsh, George, but I consider what you said to me a gift. You brought up right away what was needed. It hurt, I wish it hadn't been that way, but you helped me to confront it with us, and I needed that. Thank you, George, for the gift. I want to re-earn your trust, and that of everyone in here," she said, evidencing a quiet strength.

This was a healing comment, freely offered, in the midst of a continuing but lessening crisis. Agnes reached out and with one heartfelt thank-you had soothed and washed clean a wound, while asking for a second chance to build trust. The power of her disclosure was not lost on the group.

Bob responded, probably for many others, "Agnes, you've got my trust. I have absolutely no need to grill you over why you did what you did, even though I am curious. Maybe we can talk about that some other time. But I'm thinking here about forgiveness. I forgive what you did, and actually I feel closer to you than I ever have. It's your response to what you did that makes all the difference in the world to me. Talking about gifts, you have given me a gift today and I am very thankful."

The others shook their heads in agreement. The highly pressurized volcano had now calmed itself, leaving an atmosphere of safety and warmth that touched everyone present. George, sensing this transformation, suggested that everyone stand, hold hands, and offer a silent prayer of thanksgiving for what he termed the "wonder of the group."

The group prayer came right at the close of the session, and it was a magnificent closure indeed. Bill and Heather smiled at the group, thanked them for sharing these special moments together, and wished them well until they got together again in 1 week. As the members joyously filed out together, Bill and Heather could not help but think that confidentiality would never again be a threat to this group.

Processing

Heather and Bill decided to process the session immediately, beginning with the half-hour car ride back to the office. Simply too much had happened to delay trying to figure it out.

"I feel like I've been through a wringer!" Heather began, with a big sigh. "I don't think I've ever been part of a session with such wild swings in mood and huge shifts in direction. I was really afraid for a long time that we were going to lose the group."

Taking the big cloverleaf turn onto the interstate as he listened, Bill gratefully noticed that the traffic was uncommonly sparse for that time of day. After a demanding session like that, maybe they were going to catch a needed break. This also let him put driving a bit on "pilot" so that he could be freer to focus on their processing.

"I'm with you on all of that," Bill replied. "You know, when Agnes suddenly rushed out the door, I was literally transfixed. It kind of reminded me of Rogers in the *Journey Into Self* video years ago, where the member leaves. I found myself trying desperately to recall what the great one did then; actually, I think he let the member stay out and decide what to do. Anyway, that's not important, just that I was caught and *really* glad that you did something! How did you get to that point so fast?" he asked Heather.

"I'm not sure, Bill. I don't know, really, probably more instinct than anything else. She left, I followed, kind of stimulus-response, automatic pilot, boom-boom. I don't remember any thought about it at all. But when I got to her, she was so distraught that I felt reassured it was a good thing I'd gone. It wasn't until she began to gather herself that I suddenly thought about the group and that *I* had left it, too! I was worried about what I'd find upon returning."

"Yeah, I bet," said Bill. "And when you were both gone, I was very anxious cause I didn't have any idea how long you'd be and how everyone would handle the time. I just thought that going on with the session in your absence would be counterproductive—so, I'm not sure of it, but it seemed like they made some good use of their time. But this couldn't have gone on indefinitely. Thank goodness you came back when you did!"

"How long was it that we were gone?" Heather asked. "My sense of time just vanished."

"I think about 15 minutes or so, maybe a bit more," replied Bill. "But my sense of time was that it was l-o-n-g, nearly *eternal*." He laughed. "How's that word for a spiritually oriented group!"

Laughing with him, Heather was glad for the comic relief, however inept. As they approached the office lot, which was always crowded by midafternoon, with a note of triumph she pointed out an empty space. "There," she barked, "the other side of the yellow thing there. Get it before it's too late!" Small successes are needed at times like this. Bill parked, and they traipsed up the stairs to the office, eager to continue their processing after they both loaded up with some coffee from the trusty office pot.

"Let's see, where were we?" asked Bill. "Oh, yeah, the time issue. This group could have disintegrated here, or at several points along the way, don't you think? It was very fragile, in crisis."

"No doubt, Bill. In fact, my stomach still is knotted some about it. When that happens, I know something big has been going on. Thank goodness Agnes was able to say things to the group—and I was really impressed by her genuineness—that promoted healing. People really met her at least halfway too. That seemed like such good work to me! This was such a turnaround from where we were. It makes my head spin," she admitted.

They shared impressions about the member interactions during the latter part of the session and their amazement at the capacity of the group to save itself from disaster. They noted the use of terms by members, such as *gifts* and *forgiveness,* that they ordinarily did not hear in their groups and that they did not use themselves. They marveled at the suggestion for holding hands, followed by the group prayer. These were special and unique elements. They wondered about the role that these elements played in the growth of the group and in the ability of the members to reconnect.

Finally, Heather and Bill came to the issue of confidentiality. Even Heather, who had spent private time with Agnes, did not fully understand the details of what had happened outside the group. Maybe, the leaders questioned, they should have gotten this information out in the group and facilitated an examination of what it meant. As they talked more, they began to share some misgivings that the basic issue of confidentiality and how it was breached should have received more direct attention. Maybe, they feared, the highly positive feelings that everyone left with at the session's end might be more fleeting than real because they had not helped the group members to more fully process what had happened, what it meant, and what they had learned.

On the other hand, as Heather put it, "But we shouldn't doubt ourselves now. The trust they were expressing seemed deep and real, after all. Maybe that's enough."

"Maybe," said Bill tentatively. "But there is something else banging around inside me about all this, I'm not sure what it is." He paused reflectively. "You know, Heather, I think it's about the kind of counseling group this is, with the religious or spiritual perspective and mission of the members. Those words we talked about earlier, remember, like *forgiveness.* And the prayer. There is a power there, maybe, that—I don't know, I feel like I'm beyond my normal realm of thinking here—that goes beyond our more usual ways of dealing with problems in group, such as around confidentiality. I think I'm wondering if there is a more spontaneous kind of understanding or healing that can take place—they said it, a kind of forgiveness—that then does not demand the more detailed examination and processing of events. Boy, am I sounding weird or what?" he concluded.

"You sound mystical, or something like that, Bill," said Heather. "I can relate to it too, and I kind of like it. But it nags at me too that we haven't worked with them about reaffirming confidentiality and protecting against its infringement again. But maybe it's not necessary here."

"Yes, well, what about next session?" inquired Bill. "What should be on tap?"

"How about let's start with an open exploration of their thoughts and feelings about last week's session, now after a week has gone by?" suggested Heather. "And then wouldn't it be great if we could help them to delve into what it all meant to them, especially with regard to keeping their work confidential? Getting at the personal meaning of it all. What do you think, Bill?"

"I like it. I'm also feeling that there are some issues for me that are surfacing here, around how forgiveness and prayer fit in with my own values and way of working. Not that we would get into that during group, but I'd like to be able to work some on this with you. Are you game?"

"Only if you can listen to me too," responded Heather. "Those questions are mine also, and they're challenging. Yes, I'm game to put them on our plate for processing. I have a feeling we're going to learn a lot about ourselves during this group."

ANALYSIS

Follow the Best Practices Guidelines

Group leaders can never rest assured that the next session will be a natural extension or progression from the previous one, especially when as much as 1 week's time (or more) may intervene between sessions. Certainly, Heather and Bill rediscovered this truism during the counseling group just presented.

Group leaders must become skillful at adapting their group plan appropriately to fit changing or different conditions. Though group developmental models provide a general blueprint for what to expect, they are woefully inadequate to predict the future of any one group.

Moreover, although a group may have been evolving in a certain direction, leaders can be surprised again and again as group members take unexpected turns in the road, resulting in a next group session that seems disconnected from previous ones.

Why does the uncertain rule? Because the group and its sessions, however significant in members' lives and pervasive in effects, still takes up just a tiny relative proportion of time available in members' lives. A 2-hour weekly group session accounts for just a tad over 1% of available weekly time for each member. Therefore, lots of time exists for members to be exposed to a variety of events, experiences, thoughts, and feelings outside the group in the "real world" out there. The breach of confidentiality involving Agnes and the other members occurred in another setting. It was unpredictable and influential, producing a powerfully different set of circumstances that got acted out during the sixth session of the counseling group and for which the leaders were completely unprepared.

Utilize Group Work Competencies

Facing an unexpected crisis in the session, the leaders responded, guided largely by spontaneously made decisions. Leaders must learn to choose appropriate interventions and to apply them effectively. Were their choices the correct ones? Would alternatives, such as not following Agnes out of the group room, be preferable? Or, left with the remaining members, was Bill's choice to suspend group interaction during the absences an appropriate and effective intervention? And nearing the end of the session, was it wise for the leaders to accept without challenging the healing forces that they were observing, or should they have caused the members to purposefully examine the issue of confidentiality and its place in this group?

Of course, the "proof is in the pudding." What they did seemed to have worked. Following this pragmatic view, the leader choices made during the session appeared to keep the group intact and to propel the members forward. A crisis situation evolved into an opportunity gained.

The leaders, however, do not seem to be totally convinced about the lasting nature of this growth; they worry that it may be more ephemeral than real. This worry seems to be joined with both their fascination and their distrust of the spiritual orientation sometimes expressed by members. Could it be, they wonder, that the act of forgiveness might remove the need to process more deeply the learning and growth that may have occurred? And without such intentional processing, can anything learned be truly integrated and translated into future application? In short, might yet another break in confidentiality occur in this group because the leaders missed the opportunity presented of learning from the experience that first caused the rupture in the group?

If the leaders missed such a chance for processing during that session, might it still be possible, if they choose, to return to it at the next session? This seems to be the route that Bill and Heather are considering taking, and it may indeed be a productive one. Intentionally helping members to link their experience with derived personal meaning could be a next step for the group.

As for the leaders, it appears that the unique texture of member interactions in this group, imbued as it is at times with spiritual concepts and processes, is serving to stimulate and challenge them. They are learning about themselves more fully. Their coleader processing demonstrates the attention they give not only to events, processes, and experiences that occurred in the session ("pragmatic" processing) but also to possible deeper meanings and implications for members as well as for themselves ("deep" processing). In fact, the leaders have agreed to mutually examine how the spiritual perspective being experienced in this group may relate to their respective values and leadership styles. Such openness of group leaders to appropriately examine their personal and professional growth is exemplary and highly recommended.

QUESTIONS FOR REFLECTION AND DISCUSSION

1. During the first five sessions of this counseling group, Heather and Bill found it to be "really cooking." What goes on in a counseling group when it is functioning well? What do the members tend to do? The leaders?

2. Do you think the coleaders did enough in this group to ensure confidentiality? What do you think would generally characterize a "best practice" regarding confidentiality in counseling groups?

3. Agnes left the group room when her personal anguish became too much for her to handle. If you had been a coleader then, what would you have done? What was the range of possibilities to consider?

4. During processing, Bill revealed to Heather that his stomach had been "in knots" while she was out of the room. Group leaders are

involved with their work and develop strong affect at times. Can you relate to Bill's experience? How do you react during sessions to what is going on?

5. The Boy Scout motto is "Be Prepared." Unexpected events, sometimes crises, occur in group counseling for which preparation and knowledge of developmental theory may help but be insufficient. What else is needed, and how are you in these kinds of situations?

6. What key events did you notice occurring during this group? Were there turning points? What alternative strategies could have been tried?

CHAPTER 7

Violating the Code

BACKGROUND

For several years, Phil and Teri had co-led a semester-long counseling group for graduate students in training with the counseling psychology program at the local university. Truth be known, it was one of the highlights of their work year, something that they always looked forward to with excitement.

It wasn't that they disliked their jobs at the Family Services Center. Far from it. But working with young graduate students who were deeply involved in their preparation to become psychologists was such a blast. The students usually were eager to learn, full of energy, and invested in looking at themselves.

This kind of profile typically did not match the clients seen at the center, of course. Here, although sometimes they were interested and motivated, clients came or were referred because they were in psychological or emotional trouble. All too often, they were resistant to counseling. The work, therefore, was challenging. Not bad, just challenging. So having the opportunity to co-lead a group of healthy, bright, growth-oriented young professionals was a treat indeed, a real breath of fresh air.

It was interesting how their arrangement with the counseling psychology program had developed. Counseling groups for first-year students had been operating there for 15 years. These groups had been led in the past by their faculty. However, beginning about 7 years ago, sensitivities had emerged throughout the helping professions about "dual relationships." This term referred to conflicts that might arise from relationships between a professional helper and a client or trainee. Such dual-relationship conflicts, should they occur, are generally attributed to the professional's somehow taking advantage of the power differential existing between roles—for example, between a professor and student or between a counselor and client. In the case of professor and student, the student is dependent on the professor for evaluations and recommendations, thereby presenting the potential for an unhealthy enactment of the status differential. In the counselor-client relationship, the client is the seeker of assistance from the resource expert, again supplying the potential for exploitation of a power imbalance.

None of this is a problem unless the professor or counselor somehow takes advantage—or can be feared to take advantage—of the status differential. When this occurs, trust is violated, and the trainee or client is placed in a position of vulnerability. An alarming number of cases exist, for instance, in which therapists or professors have taken advantage of their position with vulnerable clients or students for sexual exploitation.

Sexual exploitation is not the sole reason for incorporating within ethical codes for the protection of clients, students, or subjects a prohibition against unhealthy dual relationships with professionals. According to these ethical codes, any dual relationship with clients that could impair professional judgment or increase client harm should be avoided, and if avoidance is impossible, the helper is advised to take appropriate and careful precautions to ensure that professional judgment is not abridged and that exploitation does not occur.

The counseling psychology program faculty decided to take a conservative approach regarding the dual-relationship issue and its relationship to the counseling group provided for trainees. They recognized that the potential for dual relationship abuse was present whenever their professors led counseling groups for trainees, in which student self-disclosure is a value. They identified two possible scenarios. First, the possibility existed that students might refrain from revealing personal matters in the group for fear that the professor-leader might somehow evaluate them negatively. Second, if trainees did reveal deep-seated concerns in the group, these might be used somehow against them later by the professor-leader—for example, in evaluations or recommendations.

In taking steps to avert the possibility of unhealthy dual relationships arising within the counseling group and to promote the most open environment for interaction, the faculty somewhat reluctantly decided to contract with outside experts to serve as group leaders of these experiences. This was done reluctantly because certain faculty were highly skilled group leaders with national reputations. However, the idea was that outside experts, totally unattached to any grading or evaluation process with these students, would be free from the potential dual-relationship entanglements faced by faculty. This condition then would allow for unfettered group interaction conditions to occur.

It was from this background of the dual-relationships issue that Phil and Teri were selected by the faculty to serve as coleaders of the counseling group for trainees in the counseling psychology program. They were both well-known group workers in the local mental health community, and the counseling psychology program had long enjoyed a positive working relationship with the center for which they worked, utilizing it every semester for internship placements. Teri and Phil were grateful for the opportunity to lead this group, even though it did not pay financially—just in terms of satisfaction, which always had been enough for them.

For 7 years, the purpose of the group had remained constant: to provide a safe environment through which first-year students could experience the role of group member, engage in self-disclosure and feedback, pursue personal and interpersonal concerns, and observe group leadership styles. These goals had been articulated by Dr. Larson, the faculty member in charge of group work training in the program, who had remained in the position of resource consultant to the coleaders throughout this time.

Each offering of the group had incorporated these goals. In terms of methods, the group was largely unstructured, providing members with opportunities to set their own agenda. Occasionally the coleaders would introduce an exercise or suggest that time be allotted for processing, but mostly this was run as an unstructured, confidential counseling group.

The group met for 15 weekly 2-hour sessions during the spring semester, always on Tuesdays from 4:00 to 6:00 p.m. Thus, it had become affectionately known by students and faculty alike as "the Tuesday." That's it, just "the Tuesday," probably signifying the central place it had assumed in the life of the program. All first-year students were automatically included as members in the Tuesday, a fact that was made known to them during the admissions process.

During the "Introduction to Group Work" course in fall semester, Dr. Larson further explained the upcoming group to provide additional clarification and respond to any questions or concerns, especially stressing the group's purpose, method, nonevaluative nature, and confidential status. He highlighted the difficulties that confidentiality in this intact group of cohorts can sometimes present as a way to begin sensitizing them to this important issue.

Consistent with professional ethical codes, and because the Tuesday was an opportunity for self- and interpersonal growth and not an academic experience per se, participation in it was ungraded. This condition was included and assiduously followed to remove anxiety about performance evaluation from the learning experience.

The fact that the Tuesday was an ungraded experience did not mean it was a cakewalk by any means. It loomed so large in the lives of students because of its high intensity and deeply personal nature. It was generally perceived as one of the most demanding—and most meaningful—aspects of the entire training program.

ACTION

Planning

Tradition was that sometime between Thanksgiving and the end of first semester Phil and Teri would meet with Dr. Larson to once again get oriented to the upcoming group and to renew their working relationship. They typically set aside 2 hours for a planning meeting. During this meeting, they would review plans for the group, based in part on the student evaluations from the preceding year that Dr. Larson had sent them. Part of this planning would involve a reconsideration of goals and methods and any new ideas that they might want to introduce for consideration. Dr. Larson would generally describe the new members, and they would arrange their weekly resource consultation sessions.

As the faculty member responsible for the group work training program, Dr. Larson made himself available on a weekly basis during "the Tuesday" to consult with the leaders. This was a tricky business for a couple of reasons. He was clear that supervision was not the function being provided, given the expertise and experience of Teri and Phil. Sometimes, though, separating consultation and supervision was difficult. Larson attempted to provide what he called "resource consultation"—that is, answering any questions and providing any information the leaders might need to help the group run smoothly. Second, and more important, because the group was a confidential experience, any discussions needed to occur in such a way as to protect the confidence of each member. Thus, the coleaders and consultant had worked out a communication process that protected individual confidences yet communicated about interaction patterns and group-level phenomena. Though it was sometimes cumbersome, they had found this system to work well over the years.

As they prepared to gather for their meeting with Dr. Larson, Teri and Phil met first to compare notes and explore what matters they might want to bring up with him.

"You know," began Teri, "I've been thinking about the group in light of the student evaluations. Though they seemed to really like the group last year and benefit from it, as we've discussed before, Phil, they also seemed to want more say in what happened, more control, maybe. Do you remember that?"

Phil nodded.

"So I have been wondering if what they are talking about is more collaboration," she continued. "If so, then we might try to make it even more collaborative with the members than it may have been?" She ended this thought with a rising inflection, as if asking a question or uncertain of exactly what she was trying to say.

"Not sure what you mean, Teri," replied Phil, not grasping what she meant by *collaborative* and really not wanting to fix something that he didn't think was broken in the first place. "Regale me," he invited, with a warm laugh.

"Well, I'm not sure, either," she admitted. "But I'm thinking that we've always been willing and able to work with the members, but at the same time we've called a lot of the shots, it seems to me. I mean, we've set the goals and introduced exercises when we thought they would fit, and we haven't said much about ourselves in the sessions. . . . I don't know, maybe we could just try to level the playing field even more than we have. Something like that, anyway," she ended.

This was exactly why Phil liked to work with Teri. She always brimmed with new ideas and would throw them out there, but in a nonthreatening way, very invitingly. But sometimes she could drive him absolutely nuts too, because she was never willing to leave well enough alone; she was always searching for some state of nirvana.

"Oh, Teri," he signed resignedly. "What next? You know that you can drive me crazy with these ideas of yours! Haven't we had great groups over the years, including last one? Why tamper?"

"Cause we can maybe do better. Let's make the members more like equals so we can shape the group together a bit more, let them own more of it. After all, they are all going to be group leaders, so let's get them started more. The overall group goals wouldn't need to change at all, I would think, but we could give them more of an opportunity to collaborate with us on how to accomplish them. You know, take our belief even more seriously about 'This is your group.'"

Phil responded, "Yeah, I can buy into that, certainly. The idea of ownership is important, I thought we always had been responsive to it, but—okay—let's see where it might go."

As they later explained to Dr. Larson their intent to become even more collaborative with the members, he had no problem with it, other than wondering aloud how they would actually do it. He raised this as a rhetorical question, not needing a response. But they would need to come up with the answer soon. The first session was in 3 weeks.

After some more discussions, Phil and Teri had decided to produce an enhanced collaborative climate in the group in three ways: (a) In the first session, they would very clearly include statements that "this is your group" and that their intent was to work with the members as "equals," mutually shaping what they would do and how they would do it; (b) they would participate in any exercises used, rather than restricting their involvement to introduction and processing; and (c) they would share more of themselves, as appropriate, also including their ongoing thoughts on leading the group. Thus, Teri and Phil intended to inject an ethic of collaboration into the group from the start and to become more personally involved in the sessions. They were excited about this prospect as they began the group.

Performing I

The first four sessions of the group went very well indeed. The trainees had responded enthusiastically to the heightened emphasis on collaboration. Phil and Teri were amazed at the increased energy that seemed to be generated in this group. And they very much liked what felt like a new-found freedom to be themselves more fully, less bound to the role of leader. Their group was evolving toward a situation where leadership was shared.

About the only concern they had was that one of the members, Sylvia, had been absent now for two sessions. By an agreement known to everyone involved, attendance was the only individual record that the leaders were required to report to Dr. Larson. When discussing Sylvia's first absence, Dr. Larson had advised them to "just keep an eye on it." However, after the second straight absence, he became concerned, as they did. Their concerns were deepened because no one had received an explanation from Sylvia about her absences from group. For Dr. Larson,

her absences represented larger issues surrounding commitment to training, professional behavior, and living up to program requirements. Concerns of the leaders centered on Sylvia and the group. They wondered
how she was doing and what effect her missing sessions without explanation would have on the other members. Together, the leaders and
Dr. Larson decided to give it one more week and see what happened, no
doubt hoping against hope that she would turn up back in group.

When Sylvia missed a third straight group session, all their concerns
were amplified nearly to the point of crisis. Other group members were
now becoming concerned with this matter, and against the better judgment of the leaders, it had become a topic of discussion in the session.
From that discussion, however, Teri and Phil learned from one of the
members that Sylvia had been ill for 2 weeks, missing nearly all her
classes. No other members were aware of this situation, nor, of course,
were the leaders. Why she hadn't called in to one of them to explain her
misfortune was a mystery to the leaders. For his part, Dr. Larson checked
with other professors, finding out that Sylvia had been absent from
several classes over the last 2 weeks (he did not have her for class this
semester) and that after a week or so she had called Jan, the program
secretary, to report that she had had a rough case of the flu but that she
was recovering.

Processing I

According to their schedule, Teri and Phil met with Dr. Larson
following each session, usually just to check if any of them had any needs
to be addressed. The last two meetings had been focused not only on the
excellent progress of the group but even more on the "mystery" of
Sylvia's absences from group. Now, after her third such absence, they
met with considerable anxiety.

After comparing what they had all learned about Sylvia's situation,
they began to consider the issues. The facts, as they knew them, were
that Sylvia had missed three straight group sessions without contacting
the leaders. According to group members, faculty, and Jan, Sylvia had
had the flu during most or all of this time and had missed several of her
classes, too. The leaders and members were all concerned about Sylvia.
In addition, the leaders were anxious that her absences and the increasing
group time being spent focusing on them were proving to be disruptive
to the group. Not only was Dr. Larson concerned about Sylvia; he also

questioned the quality of her professional behavior in relation to how she had handled the group absences.

Their processing of this situation was difficult and painful. Differing motivations held by the leaders and by Dr. Larson about the "Sylvia situation" served to make the conversation increasingly problematical. As they talked, it became clearer that Dr. Larson tended to view the situation in terms of the program and the profession, whereas Phil and Teri were focused on Sylvia and the group. They all agreed, though, that whatever actions taken needed to reflect a consensus decision among the three of them.

"Maybe we should call Sylvia," offered Teri, "to see how she is doing and if she is coming back to group."

"Yeah, we could do that," replied Phil. "But I'm just as concerned about the group as about Sylvia, I think. How would we handle her coming back? How would the group be affected? Some of the members are now appearing to be quite put out with how they feel Sylvia has treated them by just not showing up, as we saw last session," he said, looking at Teri.

Dr. Larson listened carefully to each comment as he was formulating his own thoughts. "This is a tough one that we all face," he observed. "I mean, you as the group leaders, and the faculty and I from the program perspective. As far as I'm concerned, not reporting in a timely way represents poor professional behavior on her part. But it's not clear to me what we should do in this case."

After talking some more, they came to action possibilities. Dr. Larson argued with increasing vigor for removing her from the group. Teri was in favor of contacting her to see if she would be able to return and, if so, for them to do what they had to do to reintegrate her within the group. Phil fell somewhere in the middle. He wanted to give priority to the coherence of the group; if Sylvia could be included in it without negatively affecting the group, then that was what he preferred.

After more exploration and analysis, accompanied by considerable reexamination, they decided to view the situation from Dr. Larson's program perspective. Sylvia had not only missed three group sessions in a row without informing the leaders but had also missed several classes without providing notification. Even though she had supposedly been ill with the flu, they all finally concurred that Sylvia probably should have exercised better professional judgment and behavior by contacting professors and the leaders appropriately.

Their decision, then, was that Dr. Larson would contact Sylvia to discuss this whole series of events in relation to missed responsibilities and that due to missing so many sessions without notification, she would be removed from the group. She would be given the option of making up the group experience next year. It was the responsibility of Teri and Phil to bring this information back to the sixth group session.

Performing II

"You did *what*?" were the first words out of Jill, one of the more vocal group members. "This is just incredible!"

Others in the group were clearly in agreement. The sudden burst of indignation caught Teri and Phil totally by surprise. They had gone into the session fully expecting that the members would understand the reasoning behind their decision to remove Sylvia from the group. In fact, they had assumed this would be welcomed by the members, remembering how some of them had expressed dismay at how Sylvia had handled her absences. Furthermore, the coleaders had entered the session with a sense of confidence in the decision, due to the processing they had engaged in previously with Dr. Larson. Therefore, the unexpected reaction of the members was immobilizing at first.

Feeling under attack, Phil decided that he would explain again why Sylvia had been removed from the group. Maybe they had left something important out earlier, he reasoned.

"We talked with Dr. Larson about this at length," he reiterated. "Finally, it seemed to the three of us that the fairest thing to do for Sylvia, as well as the group, was to arrange with her to withdraw and pick group up again next time. In this way—"

He did not get the thought finished. Boom! There was a cascade of interruptions. Landon's words captured the theme: "Yes, we heard it the first time. But the crux of the problem is that you did not ask *us*. What was all your talk from the beginning that this was *our* group, and stuff like that? When there was a really important decision to be made, we were nowhere in sight. I feel betrayed."

Billie Jo followed Landon's strongly put message. "That's exactly what I'm wondering, Phil and Teri! Where is the collaboration when it counts? Whose group is this, anyway? Dr. Larson's?"

The challenge contained in these words was unmistakable. And it was unnerving to the coleaders.

A silence fell on the room. Members had discharged their anger at being left out of an important decision that was made. The leaders had been listening, trying to understand what was behind the members' intense feelings, trying to manage their own, and, right now, grappling with what to do.

Teri and Phil had had many successful group-leading experiences, including several with this very group. It passed through their minds that never before had they ever been so challenged—no, make that attacked— as right now. It did not feel good; in fact, it hurt.

They also realized in a flash that of course the group members were absolutely correct. The leaders and even Dr. Larson had blown it by completely overlooking the role of the group in the decision that was reached. And, most embarrassing of all, this oversight had occurred in *this* group, the one in which Teri and Phil had emphasized collaboration with members. Now this group's very existence was compromised.

These thoughts, and more, were pulsating quickly through each leader. Immediately before Teri and Phil was the question of what to do now. Enmeshed with this question was their confusion about their independence in taking action versus the role of Dr. Larson and what he would think of this situation.

Teri began. "Phil and I have worked together long enough that I can tell from his facial expressions alone that he is as bowled over about this as I am." Checking with Phil, she asked, "Am I right, Phil?" Quickly, Phil responded, "Absolutely. I'm feeling very much under the gun here."

"Well, then, let me try to go on," offered Teri. Looking at the group, she said, "I very much appreciate you being straight with us about your feelings. You have been very responsible about that. At the same time, your feedback is difficult to take, but I'm trying to cope. Back to responsibility: Maybe you have been more responsible than we have been with you. We—well, maybe I should just speak for me here, I—just missed the whole important thing you have brought out. In our intention to do what we thought was the right thing here about Sylvia's absences, I admit it, we missed your part in this. This was especially wrong, as Landon and Billie Jo said, when collaboration had been placed front and center in our group. Where we go from here, I guess, is the real question so we can recover our good working relationship."

"Yes, well said, Teri," added Phil. "We missed it, and I apologize for that," he admitted with a sigh. "It was a mistake, a costly one. Can we get back on track?" he asked, looking around the group.

Predictably, Jill responded for the group. "I want to thank you for acknowledging the mistake and to underline that yes, it was a *very* big one. The question I have—I don't know about the others—is, Where do you go from here? What about Sylvia? Where will our input go now? Is it too late? Then what? I think a lot depends on answers to those kinds of questions. I think it comes down to the basic question of 'Whose group is this?' "

"Let's spend the last—let's see," Teri said, glancing at her watch, "15 minutes we have here today talking about your input, can we? Given all that we know about Sylvia's absences and the group's development, what would you recommend be done?" she asked the group.

After some discussion, it was apparent the members were in agreement that if Sylvia were feeling better and could come back the next week, she should do so. The sentiment, summarized by Billie Jo, was, "She's a part of us in all other ways; we'll work with her here if she can return."

Realizing that time was just about over for this session, Phil attempted to conclude with "Okay, looks like we'll need to carry over until next session, due to time. Also, as you know, we will need to meet with Dr. Larson to discuss this whole matter. We will present your feelings and position on this to him. The good news is that I don't think he has yet been able to talk with Sylvia."

Much more could have been said and should have been said. It seemed that members had some feeling about Dr. Larson and his role, for instance. But time was up, and everyone was drained anyway. Leave it till next time.

Processing II

Phil and Teri talked briefly right after the session about next steps. They did not have much time to spend. But they quickly decided that one of them should call Dr. Larson right away to ask him to hold on contacting Sylvia until the three of them had their weekly consultation meeting. Phil placed the call, got the message tape, and left as clear a message as he could.

At their next meeting, Dr. Larson began by asking about the phone call. "Of course, I didn't speak with her until our meeting, as you asked, Phil. In your phone message, you mentioned something about the importance of the last group session. Shall we discuss that?" he asked the two of them.

"Oh, yes, we should," they responded, nearly in unison.

"Sounds like a lot of energy around that question!" noted Dr. Larson. "Something big must have happened. Well, let's get started."

Teri and Phil described the session, noting the important group processes that had occurred. It did not take them long at all to get to what they both felt was the crux of the issue: the sense of betrayal felt by the members, resulting from the decision made by the three of them to remove Sylvia from the group, and, of course, the members' preferring that Sylvia be allowed back into the group if she was able.

"Yes, and one of them, who, I think, was speaking for many in the group, really challenged us about whose group it was, even wondering if it was yours," said Teri to Dr. Larson.

"Ouch!" uttered Dr. Larson. "That one really gets me. It reminds me of something Carl Rogers once said to a client about her pain 'cutting like a knife.' Well, all three of us seem to be in this soup together, don't we."

"Let's see if I have it right," he began to summarize. "Essentially, the members feel betrayed because of our independent decision about Sylvia—our failure to involve them in it. And this is especially important to them because of the value of collaboration you previously established together. And they want her back in the group, not removed. Is that close?" he asked.

"You've got the gist of it. All except the anger and resentment. When you say it, it all sounds so logical and controlled. It wasn't that way in the group!" said Phil.

"I know, and I apologize if I sounded as if all this was just easy stuff. It isn't, and I'm feeling troubled by it too," confessed Dr. Larson. "In fact, maybe it would be a good idea if we talk some about how we are feeling and what might be emerging from the experience. How does that sound?"

"That would be great," said Teri, "because Phil and I haven't yet had a chance to do this. And, as you say, we are in this one together, so taking the time here for all of us to do this seems important."

So their level of processing deepened to include their feelings, values, and the meaning they were drawing from the experience surrounding Sylvia's situation.

Dr. Larson began by extending his reference to Rogers' "cuts like a knife" phrase that he had used earlier. "This perception that the group is mine really hits me hard," Dr. Larson said. "I mean, I have always tried to behave just the opposite! I have gone extra lengths to distance myself from the experience, to be sure that confidences were kept, to serve as a supportive resource only. So to have this come back to me in this way is galling." He paused. "I'm realizing I have quite a bit of anger about this, which surprises me. But it's there just the same. Well, let that sit for awhile, and let's just hear from each of us, how would that be?"

The other two agreed because each of them was full of feeling.

Teri went next. "I guess being seen as a betrayer is absolutely the last thing I would ever want. Losing the trust of the group is so threatening to me, and I've found it just difficult to sleep, even, since that session. You know, my self-confidence is kind of shaky right now."

Phil reached out and placed his hand gently on his coleader's shoulder, saying, "This really is hurtful for you, Teri, and for me, too, but I know we'll get through this together."

Looking at Phil, Teri realized, once again, how she valued him as a colleague. She let him know with a sigh: "Thanks, Phil, I needed that, I guess. Thanks for your support."

"No problem, Teri," he said, "and I need yours just as much. Wow, this was a difficult session! Everything had been going so well, the group and us working so beautifully together. Maybe conflict was to be expected around some issue, any issue. Maybe the situation with Sylvia simply supplied that issue. Or maybe it was much more than that. I don't know, but as usual, for me, I think it is probably somewhere in the middle between those two possibilities. At any rate, I don't know just how I'm feeling about this. I think probably embarrassment is a large part of it, also something like a feeling of recklessness, as if we did something that was not carefully enough thought through. I'm certain that we all made a very big error, though, when we left the group out in the cold. They should have been right there with us making the decision."

"I am aware that I kind of pressured you both to give some priority to the program versus, I guess, the student and the group," offered Dr. Larson. "While in retrospect that may not have been wise, still program considerations are important here. In fact, never before have I sensed so acutely the kind of conflict that can occur between the program and the group. No doubt this conflict contributed to our decision."

"Yeah, I felt that tension, and it did influence me," said Teri. "But what gets to me even more strongly is that not once did we ever catch ourselves to say, 'Well, what would the group members say about this?' or to wonder something like 'Shouldn't we involve the members in our decision?' So I think to myself now, 'What in the world were we thinking?' "

Teri's questions seemed to hit the nail on the head for all of them, attested to by their silence.

Dr. Larson broke in first. "As I ruminate about what you just said, Teri, I, too, am caught with no answer. I now believe we should have done that in some way. And I'm thinking that a large part of the anger I was expressing earlier might be traced to my sense that I—and we—but certainly I should have been smart enough to have realized that need. So I am kind of kicking myself for my own stupidity or arrogance or, I don't know what."

As they talked in this deeply personal way, the level of anxiety in the room began to drop. They had confronted their experience directly, worked through strong feelings, and learned. They were beginning to move toward a resolution.

"Well, I'm wondering where we are now with this situation," said Dr. Larson. "Might we test the waters some?"

"Yes, I think so," said Teri. "Actually, I'm feeling much better now than when we began today." She looked at Phil, inviting him to reply.

"Me, too," agreed Phil. "I think we've covered lots of ground and made some progress. I'm ready to talk about what to do now. In fact, here's what I think: Teri and I should approach Sylvia. Find out how she's doing, tell her that the group misses her and hopes she can return, maybe find out something about why she didn't contact us. Then, if she's ready to come back, we can help her get back into the group. What does that sound like?"

"Man, that came out easily!" marveled Teri. "But, yes, I think that sounds good." She smiled. "It's in keeping with the group members' wishes and is respectful of Sylvia. What do you think, Dr. Larson?"

Dr. Larson was thinking that this probably was the way to go, to put the group and Sylvia first over any program or professional behavior considerations. Those considerations still gnawed at him, as if this solution did not get at all of it. But maybe, he decided, it was a price to pay for the kind of working arrangement that had been created.

"Yeah, I agree. Why don't you try it? This whole discussion has shown me how the group must come first here and how I need to keep way out of it with program concerns. Also, I am really aware of how we erred by not remembering the group and its proper role—and of how we can turn around a poor decision, hopefully leading to a better outcome. Well, we'll see about that, won't we? Good luck to you. I'll be real interested in how it goes."

Performing III

It went well, very well indeed. Sylvia reentered the group. She explained her illness and apologized for not contacting the leaders. The members helped her to get back in by doing what they said they would do: They brought her up to date as best they could, devoting almost the entire session to that task. Finally, toward session's end, they addressed the process they had all been through.

Teri said to the group as a whole, "Well, we have been through an awful lot during the last 2 weeks. As I look around, I see that we are back again, intact as a group after Sylvia's absence over a few sessions. And we struggled to get back to this point." She let that fall to see if anyone would pick up next.

Jill did. "Whew!" She blew out air in a blast. "Yes, we've been through a whole lot, and it felt risky too. I'm feeling renewed, I think, since you and Phil reversed your decision to let the group into it. Coming back today to this session, especially with Sylvia here, has felt very healing to me."

Others followed up with similar positive comments. The group was reestablishing itself.

Phil, in concluding the session, said, "One of the things that was shown, I think, is that leaders can make mistakes and learn from them—with the group's help. You helped us to see our error—that in a real sense we had violated the code of collaboration that we had established among ourselves. It wasn't pretty, but we got the message, and I hope you feel we responded. This was a real important experience for me, and I am thankful for you to help it happen. I am excited, again, about the next half of the group that stretches ahead of us. See you all next week."

ANALYSIS

Follow the Best Practice Guidelines

This case develops within the ongoing context of the dual-relationship dilemma facing the helping professions today. The conflict that emerges around Sylvia's absences exemplifies confusions existing between considerations attached to the program and to the group itself. Demonstrated is the importance of being aware of the professional context within which one is operating as a group leader and being able to respond accordingly.

The concern with harmful dual relationships has led training programs to give increased attention to faculty-student relationships as well as to personal growth experiences that are offered by programs for their students. Some programs have adopted group training approaches similar to Dr. Larson's, above, where faculty are separated from the experience to enhance freedom in student exploration. Other programs have sanctioned their faculty to function as group leaders with students if the faculty take responsible precautions to ensure that appropriate professional standards and ethical guidelines are met.

Further, the case shows how the leaders, in tandem with Dr. Larson, found themselves operating in a vacuum in deciding what to do regarding a group member's absences. Though they engaged in a useful processing among themselves in reaching a decision, they committed what turned out to be a serious error of omission: They failed to take into account the will of the group. They reached their decision totally independently of group member input, and it proved especially costly in this group, in which a collaborative ethic had been mutually developed. Thus, when a major decision was made, it was reached completely outside a collaborative process. The group members called the leaders on it by asking pointedly whose group this was.

At this point, the group was in crisis, with its very existence in jeopardy. The leaders were caught with a decision made not just by them but also in conjunction with the faculty representative and resource consultant.

Utilize Group Work Competencies

Phil and Teri's ability to work with Dr. Larson in processing this situation led to a successful resolution. Their processing moved from an analysis of group events and experiences—what I call "pragmatic processing"—to examining openly their respective feelings, values, and derived meaning. This latter type of processing, which I term "deep processing," led them to reexamine their previous position of removing the member from the group and construct a new approach that incorporated group member input. In addition, the leaders were able to model effective leader behavior in the group, demonstrating genuineness and the capacity for appropriate self-confrontation. The members appreciated the candor of the leaders and their willingness to be fallible.

In sum, the case shows how leaders can make a mistake and, with deep processing, be able to learn from it, converting what would have been a failure into a success. In this case, the violated code of collaboration, once transgressed, could be renewed so that the group could move forward.

QUESTIONS FOR REFLECTION AND DISCUSSION

1. Dual relationships are of ethical concern in counseling and the helping professions. How does the counseling group case examined in this chapter connect with the "dual-relationship" issue? How was it handled? What alternatives might exist? How will you deal with dual relationships in the groups that you lead?

2. If you were Dr. Larson, what issues would you have been aware of in working with Phil and Teri? With regard to Sylvia? What kinds of ground rules might you set?

3. If you were Sylvia, how might you have felt about the decision that was made? How about the group members?

4. What does collaboration of group leaders and members mean? In your opinion, was there a violation of the understanding when Sylvia was removed from the group? What would you have done, do you think?

5. The coleaders engaged in both pragmatic and deep processing. Explain the differences. How did these forms of processing contribute to sustaining the group? Have you ever been involved in deep processing? What was it like?

PART V

Psychotherapy Groups

Cartoon by J. C. Conyne. Used with permission.

Garpp, the Psychotherapy
Group Leader

By now, you may rightfully be feeling sorry for George but admiring his perspicacity! Garpp has no doubt become in your mind's eye an inept and hapless group leader, representing, (hopefully) in an extreme form, how group leaders can go wrong.

Cartoon by J. C. Conyne. Used with permission.

Group psychotherapy is premised on a variety of therapeutic factors, including universality, the factor being addressed above. Group members often receive solace from realizing, maybe for the first time, that they are not alone with problems but that there are others who experience similar ones. Garpp's insensitive response to George violates this sense of universality and, as well, communicates an undesirable absence of respect and acceptance.

Good psychotherapy group leaders seek to build cohesion, or a sense of connectedness, in their groups as a precursor to therapeutic change. Our bumbling Garpp erred badly by his nontherapeutic response to George in the above example. A preferred response might have been simply: "Of course, you are an important part of us, George."

Cartoon by J. C. Conyne. Used with permission.

CHAPTER 8

Problems With Diversity

BACKGROUND

The Crossroads Center was located in the heart of the inner city. Since it had first opened its doors 5 years ago, the center had been flooded by clients, or "consumers," as they are known in the mental health system. The consumers were drawn from the local neighborhood and included both residents and transients.

The neighborhood, known as "Crossroads," was an original part of the city and at one time was the center of city life. However, over the last century the economic and social conditions had changed dramatically. For the last quarter-century, Crossroads had become the locus of high crime, homelessness, and depressed real estate.

During the last 10 years, a wave of "neighborhood revitalization" had emerged, consistent with the bigger theme of "rebuilding downtown" that was becoming increasingly common in major cities across the country. This new plan was spearheaded by a mixed coalition of political, cultural, and entrepreneurial interests. At the same time, the resurgence was opposed by an equally eclectic but different coalition of political, preservationist, and social advocacy groups who were concerned that what they called the "gentrification" initiative would result in tearing down architecturally significant buildings and displacing residents from their homes.

The Crossroads Center was established within this social, political, and economic ferment to provide quality service to local residents and transients. As such, it had become a welcome addition to the community, though not at first. As the center was a branch of the regional mental health center system and was staffed by licensed mental health professionals, the first few months of its existence were met with distrust by many local residents.

Over time, however, the center staff was able to earn trust and respect by taking active steps in becoming involved in community life. The center even developed a reputation for social advocacy as it sought to influence changes and support programs that would lead to improved social and economic conditions.

Its ongoing consultations with the local police district related to the handling of domestic disputes had proven to be effective and respected by police personnel involved, although not well known among the community. However, two other programs had made the center a strong community presence. The center's high-stakes crisis intervention consultation three summers before to help resolve heightened tensions among the police, business owners, and minority youth in a central gathering point of the Crossroads area had received front-page media attention and been greatly appreciated on all sides. And its organization of city agencies to jointly sponsor the Summer Festival for Crossroads Youth had emerged as the big hit of the summer season in the Crossroads. Not lost among Crossroads community leaders was the insistence by center staff that the leaders be included on the festival planning committee. Thus, the center's credibility as an important community agency was rising.

Of course, the provision of quality, appropriate mental health services was the primary mission of the center. Not too surprisingly, the legitimacy arising from becoming involved and helpful with some of the ongoing real-life issues of the community had had the effect of increasing the demand for mental health service.

In addition to case management services and family intervention, the center staff had decided, as a matter of policy, that the preferred mode of treatment would be in the form of groups. They had taken this position for several reasons.

First, the center director, Dr. Sally Ferguson, known as "Fergie" to her staff and friends, held a strong belief that group-based interventions were at least as effective as others, including individual counseling and psychotherapy. In fact, the Crossroads Center had been founded on this belief in group treatment. That is, Crossroads was a "test case," designated by the local mental health board as the site for experimenting with group treatment as a primary delivery approach. Over the last few years, Dr. Ferguson had been pleased to note in the professional literature the mounting research studies attesting to the effectiveness and efficacy of group therapy as a helping modality.

A second important and related reason for the center's adopting group treatment as a main delivery vehicle was that the center had also been targeted by the local mental health board to experiment with providing cost-effective services. The idea was that those that worked would be generalized to other branches of the system in an effort to more broadly reduce costs associated with mental health delivery. This approach also could be readily justified to third-party payers within the managed-care system as being especially cost-effective, which translated into more insurance reimbursements for consumers. In addition, providing most services through groups would make the acquisition of mental health services more possible for consumers, as the service cost per consumer hour would be reduced.

Third, and most important to the center staff, was their premise that the "collectivist" orientation of group approaches would generally fit the life orientation of most of its consumers, who were African American, Hispanic, and, to a lesser extent, Asian. In these cultures, interdependence tends to be preferred over independence. It was hypothesized by staff, then, that the concept of the "circle" in group therapy and other group approaches might resonate with the dominant cultural preference of members of the racial and ethnic groups seeking services at the center. In fact, a rousing debate had taken place on the mental health board, back when the center was first being proposed, about what the center's name would be. Dr. Ferguson, the center's only director throughout its existence and a prime architect of its creation, had taken—and lost—the position that its title should be "The Circle" in order to emphasize its collectivist philosophy and group-oriented approaches. This was probably the only argument Fergie had lost in the last 5 years.

A big one that Fergie didn't lose had to do with staff demographics. She thought it was critically important that staff not only be well trained but also reflect the dominant and enduring demographic characteristics of the Crossroads catchment area. As a result, at Crossroads, just 10% of the professional staff were Caucasian, and 25% were male. At the Crossroads Center, diversity was a way of life.

So the Crossroads Center was a place of experimentation located in a geographic area of dynamic change. This mixture made for interesting times, which, as the Chinese say, can also be a curse.

All therapy groups at Crossroads were brief, and most consumers entered them through agency referral or on their own, due to some present crisis in their lives. Issues being faced frequently had a strong situational component, linked to such problems as unemployment, family violence, substance abuse, and homelessness. Usually associated with these situational factors might be any number of mental, emotional, and/or psychological dysfunctions, including depression, anxiety, anger and aggression, and sometimes psychoses. At times, also, consumers who sought service were basically intact psychologically but were going through a severe life transition, such as a broken relationship, in which the ensuing stress was beyond their present coping resources.

Center practice had been to endorse heterogeneity in forming groups, a position that emerged directly from its strong philosophy upholding the value of diversity. This meant that demographic, situational, and psychological factors, as well as level of functioning, were mixed. Group composition, therefore, always included a rich variety of characteristics, experiences, goals, and challenges. Heterogeneity was adopted as a strategy of group formation at the center for several reasons. It produced a social microcosm in the groups that mirrored the diverse conditions of the larger Crossroads community, which was considered desirable. It allowed for quicker placement of consumers into group treatment, as the organizational arrangements for starting the groups were not complicated. Finally, it allowed for testing the center's experimental group therapy approach in its most liberal heterogeneous form, outside artificial attempts to control for presenting conditions and problems.

However, staff had become increasingly concerned about their group therapy program. It seemed that dropout rates had been growing, and leaders reported that the sessions too often seemed either tedious or unmanageable. There was a growing suspicion that the prized heterogeneity on which the groups were based needed to be examined. Cognizant of this situation, Chaunston and Tabitha met to plan their next group.

ACTION

Planning

Chaunston and Tabitha had been staff counselors at Crossroads since its beginning 5 years ago. In fact, they had been the first African American hires there and had enjoyed the opportunity to work with Fergie to shape the center. Strong endorsers of the "circle" philosophy and its emphasis on heterogeneity, they were now among those staff who were questioning if changes should be made—not so much in the emphasis of the center on the group approach as on the procedures used to produce heterogeneity among members.

They sat down to plan their next psychotherapy group. This, in itself, was somewhat of a novelty. As had been the practice at Crossroads, planning of groups was not a priority. Really, there was no need for devoting much effort to planning groups, for they tended to be set up the same way: as 15-session groups aiming to maximize diversity among members and to help members manage their lives better. Intakers took pains to ensure, as much as possible, that each group would be balanced to include both genders, representative races and ethnic groups, a range of presenting situational problems, and varying psychological and emotional disorders and conditions.

"I think it's time we try some other way," began Tabitha. "Our last group was pretty much a nightmare, if you remember, Chaunston. And I don't think it was us. I think there was simply way too much difference!"

"Remember?" he replied ruefully, rolling his eyes. "How could I ever forget! We had two manic-depressives, an antisocial guy who threatened all of us, a really normal middle-aged woman who was dealing with grief, and almost a small race war breaking out from week to week. Yeah, I remember! It was really tough."

"In the first few years, basing our groups on diversity seemed to work well, sometimes great," observed Tabitha. "I don't know, maybe the extremes of diversity, especially in terms of sickness, have just gotten to be too wide and deep in the Crossroads. I really mean it. Pathology is just mushrooming. We've talked about this a lot in staff, right?" Chaunston nodded. "Maybe that's it, and maybe we should always have put more brakes on, tried to set stuff up more intentionally. What do you think?" she asked him.

"Well, it's been a grand experiment, hasn't it," Chaunston stated. "I mean, Fergie just wanted to go that way, a matter of principle, of faith. There's backing for going the way of heterogeneity, but there are contrary views that we should probably begin taking seriously—like homogeneity, as a counter. Like Yalom said—we all know this—the first order of business for forming a group should always be to promote cohesion. I think this is what you, and we all for the last year or so, have been addressing."

"Hmm, yes, probably," mused Tabitha. "I've sensed that it's sometimes awfully hard to find a way to pull members together, to get them to connect. And when it doesn't happen, then we get into dropout problems and other difficulties."

"Yeah, Tabitha," went on Chaunston. "And regarding group dropouts, haven't they been a problem almost from the beginning, anyway? As I've thought about it, not only have members sometimes found it hard to find things in common, but often they haven't seemed to understand what a group was or what was expected of them in group therapy. This is a different problem, I know. And then more problems, like a surprising number, at least to me, of members over the years have requested to be seen individually. And then it seems that more regularly, leaders— including me—have complained that their groups are becoming places to "keep a lid on," remote from any therapeutic benefit. On occasion, aggressive behavior in the group has erupted—you remember it did in our last group—without our being able to work it through properly. We even had to remove members from that group for inappropriate behavior, remember?"

"Dang, are you long-winded," teased Tabitha. "Now that you have analyzed the situation, Dr. Freud, do you agree with me or not? Should we try something different?"

"Hey, woman!" he shot back. "Usually you're the one who rattles on and on. Maybe I've caught your disease." He laughed. "Oh, all right, fair enough. I'll cease and desist. But, yes, yes, I think we need to alter how we are doing our therapy groups. Case closed."

"No, no, not so fast, Dr. Freud," she persisted. "I need you in this mode now more than ever. How do you suggest we change things?"

"Okay, I'll go along with this if you stop 'Freuding' me!" he said, making a face. "Look, to me it's becoming simple. We try to cut down on the variety. Now, I know this flies in the face of all that we are supposed to uphold as a center, but the times they are a-changin'. Uh, oh, now don't start calling me Dylan!" And he laughed.

"No, I'm through flattering you," she said, smiling. "I like that idea of cutting down the variety. Where do we start? Let's see. . . . What are the sources of variety? Let's identify them."

"Okay, that's cool," said Chaunston. "We've got diverse member demographic characteristics like race, gender, age; different presenting situations; a range of emotional and psychological problems. What else is there?"

"I'm just thinking of another factor, a thought I got from the conference on brief group therapy I went to last week, which was great, I think I told you," said Tabitha. "We have been trying to work with these differences all within a pretty short time frame, like 10 to 15 two-hour sessions. Maybe there's not enough time to do all this, so time can be a factor to consider."

"Yes, good point. But with time, we'd be looking at increasing sessions, not decreasing. A different direction."

"Yes, I wonder how that would be viewed by Fergie?" asked Tabitha. "Or, any of this, anyway?" She shook off her doubt and plunged ahead. "Something else to consider, it was emphasized, is to select and prepare prospective members for the group. We've been talking some about selection and maybe making some changes, but maybe we should also consider preparation."

"And the list goes on," added Chaunston. "We always have been—not just us but the whole staff, I'm sure—quite unstructured in our therapy groups. This is another whole different issue to consider. If we were to become more focused within the sessions, this might influence members to be more intentional, too. But hey, we are really spinning off here, like into the ozone. We can't do all of this, and maybe we shouldn't do any of it, I don't know! Rein us in, Tabitha, will you?" he implored, only half jokingly.

"But I was liking this, because, you know, since we got our whole therapy group program going 5 years ago, we haven't spent much time at all like this, questioning what we were doing and how we were doing it. This feels overdue to me—how about you?"

Chaunston paused. She's right, he thought. Maybe I'm missing the value of what we're doing, with trying to pick something to get done.

"I guess you're right," he said. "I'm just in a hurry. Thanks for catching me."

They then proceeded to discuss the various options they had generated, analyzing which one or ones they might be able to alter for their upcoming therapy group and which could be approved by Fergie.

"The one thing that would never get past Fergie," insisted Tabitha, "is to move away from our charge for our groups to reflect the race and ethnicity of Crossroads itself. That's a deadbolt lock, we know that, and we agree with it, too. Right?" she checked with Chaunston.

He nodded, as if to say, "Sure, absolutely."

"Well, given all that," went on Tabitha, "what if we think about limiting the range of situational problems that people come in with? We could do this by setting up a therapy group focused on a content area, not open to any kind of content. For instance, let's see, we could set up a group for substance abuse therapy, or for grief, or domestic violence, or, umm, anger management. To focus the content. What do you think?" she asked Chaunston.

"Yes!" he replied with enthusiasm. "This is just what I was thinking! Great minds think alike. Let's do it."

"Good. It's just the kind of step I think we need to take. We've been inundated with substance abuse issues lately, Chaunston, I've really noticed that. How about doing a group on substance abuse therapy and seeing how that goes?"

"Okay, wow, never seen such excitement about work!" laughed Chaunston. "That sounds fine with me, a good choice. And we've certainly had experience working with substance abusers here. So how do we get to that point? What do we need to do?"

"You know that we'll need to get Fergie's approval. This would be the first such group here, as we both know. But I kind of think she'll agree, cause she knows that something is missing here. And if we can show her that diversity is still very much a part of all this—and it is, cause we'll still have differing demographics and levels of functioning—I just know she'll go for it, too," said Tabitha. "But after that we'll need to work out the procedures for getting staff to refer to the group and the intakers to assign to it. It might be best to begin this new group just internally, not trying to advertise or market it outside the center to others until we've had some positive experience with it first."

They discussed these necessary next steps, developing what they thought was a workable plan of action. Only 3 weeks remained until the group was slated to begin, so not much time was available to make many changes. After obtaining Fergie's blessing, their plan involved meeting with the staff and intakers to explain the "new" group and how it would operate, as well as what sort of prospective members might be suitable for it. Tabitha and Chaunston were off and running, breaking new ground, and feeling good about their change in direction, even while holding their breath about its viability.

Happily, consistent with the experimental climate that always had characterized the center, after careful discussion Fergie and the staff supported the changes and worked toward making them happen. The substance abuse therapy group was to be viewed as an "innovative pilot study." Results from the group would be used to help staff evaluate if moving more in this direction of focused group therapy would be advisable. Although the pilot test status of the group added some extra pressure to the undertaking, the leaders were grateful for the support.

Efforts to fill the new group had yielded seven members. Two from present caseloads were African American women. Three were newly assigned through intake, including one Hispanic American male adolescent (Raul), a white middle-aged woman (Betty), and an African American female adolescent (Doreen). These five were all dealing with substance abuse issues.

The remaining two members had been assigned to the group before it had been altered to focus on substance abuse. Looking into their records, the leaders learned that these consumers had no apparent substance abuse problem. Anthony, who was a white 19-year-old, had been referred to the center for "anger outbursts." Maxine, the second member, was a 35-year-old African American woman who was grieving over the suicide of her daughter 8 weeks ago. Her clinical profile showed her to be withdrawn and deeply depressed at a level beyond that usually expected with developmental grief. However, the leaders decided it was too late to switch these consumers out of the group, and there was no other group option available then, so they were kept.

As was center practice, all prospective members completed an assessment battery before the group, consisting of a standard demographic and personal questionnaire and the MMPI-2. Because of the lack of time, it was not possible to meet with these consumers beforehand. This troubled the leaders, as they had hoped to change typical center practice by including a preparation meeting.

For these and other uncountable reasons, as the first session approached, the leaders' prior excitement now bordered on anxiety. There were so many unknowns. What, they wondered to each other, would happen?

Performing

They had made it to the sixth session (of 15). It had not been easy. After Session 2, Maxine had stopped coming to the group after not having said much more than her name in the group. When a worried Tabitha called her following the second absence, the member patiently and sadly explained that the group just didn't meet her needs: "All you ever talked about was drinking and drugs. And so much anger! I felt attacked because I'm black!" she said, with deep sadness, "and I couldn't deal with that. So I left. I just want my daughter back."

Tabitha was deeply affected by Maxine's reason for leaving. Of course, she had witnessed Anthony's behavior, which she took as rude and needing to be addressed. But somehow she had missed its racial significance. Tabitha decided that she needed to be much more attentive to this dynamic. Fortunately, with just a little work, she was able to arrange to see Maxine for individual therapy and to refer her to a community grief support group.

Up to that point, interactions in the group had been characterized by expressions of confusion by all members about what the group was all about and what they should be doing, silent resistance to participation, explosive outbursts, and monopolization of available group time. The resistance was shown by all the members who had been diagnosed with substance abuse problems, and it was wrapped up in denial. This dynamic was not unexpected and could be worked with through earning of trust, generation of cohesion among members, and constructive leader confrontation. But whenever therapeutic movement appeared to be building, Anthony would seem to take over the group, alternating between dominating the time available through telling long, self-centered stories and by attacking and belittling other members. His racist verbiage had ceased after Maxine's departure. At the sixth session, however, it explosively returned and was directed at the leaders.

Members had been stuck for a while but were discussing in a fairly productive way what was accounting for that condition. Suddenly, Anthony spat out angrily, "You are absolutely worthless bags of shit!" as he glared first at Chaunston and then at Tabitha. "It's just what my daddy always told me. You blacks couldn't lead a fart from a paper bag! Nothing's ever gonna get done in here! I'm outta here, and don't come after me, either!" And with that, he got up and stalked out of the room, slamming the door behind him.

In one fell swoop, Anthony had verbally butchered the leaders and all African American people and then cut and run. No doubt this was a fairly often used style of his.

Betty, the remaining white person in the group, immediately broke into tears and couldn't speak. The others seemed surprisingly unmoved, as if all this wasn't news to them. While Betty softly cried, Raul, the Hispanic American, said to the others, "Hey, man, I feel for you, but, you know, we've *all* been through this before, and it don't mean nothin', you know?" The African American members, nearly as one, just sighed, shrugged, and looked at the leaders, as if to say, "Are you all right?"

Tabitha and Chaunston were wounded but not mortally. They too had been there before with this kind of racial attack, but it had been a long time since anything like this had ever happened in one of their groups.

Tabitha chose to focus on Betty, who had now stopped weeping, rather than her own feelings. "Betty, you were really affected by what Anthony did. Can you tell us about that?" she asked gently.

Betty nodded. "Yeah, I'm just so ashamed of him. More than that, I'd like to kill him! No, I don't mean that, not really, just make him take it back, say something good to you. We don't need this stuff. My ex was like that, I learned after not too damn long, and I just couldn't take it, probably one reason I got into drinking so bad. But that's over with, I want to move on. But," she said, looking at Tabitha, "there's no place for that race stuff, and I'm so sorry it happened."

"Thank you, Betty," replied Tabitha, meaning it. Betty's genuine expression of sadness and regret warmed the previously chilled room. "How about the rest of you?" she asked, checking to see how the other African American members—who also had been attacked—were doing.

After some discussion, Doreen, one of those members, seemed to speak for them all when she said, "I'll take Betty any day over that trash! I'm glad he's gone, good riddance, don't want him back. Maybe it'll be better now."

A brief silence took hold. Everyone looked at the leaders. Tabitha and Chaunston knew they needed to respond to the attack on them by Anthony.

Chaunston began. "I'm glad you are all doing okay with what happened here. It was ugly, real ugly. Let me tell you my thoughts." He slowly expelled air. "I don't mind being challenged sometimes by group members. It's really fine; it's often a way I can learn too. What got me here, though, was being put down and attacked because I am an African American! It hurt me and still does. But I take comfort in how all of you handled this, I really do. *You* have helped me a lot. I think that attack was probably more Anthony's problem than mine, certainly, and we can all grow as a group through this. Still, I wish it hadn't happened, that this kind of blind hatred due to race no longer faced any of us."

He looked at Tabitha, whose eyes seemed to be glistening with tears. "Chaunston," she said to him directly, talking across the group, "really, I don't know if I could have managed here without you being here, too." She looked at the group and smiled through her tears. "And *you*. You have meant a lot to me today. I don't want to dismiss the crassness of those words we heard—that attack on us—but you know, it seems that we can move on now, do some good work cause we are more together."

Interestingly, a feeling of calm seemed to spread across the group, including the leaders. Though the leaders realized they would need to check back with Anthony later, implicitly they and all the members seemed to grasp that now the group was their own.

Processing

Immediately following the session, the leaders met for processing. They were emotionally spent, but they felt renewed by the group members' response to Anthony's racist rage.

"I haven't been attacked personally for my blackness since I was in college!" said Chaunston. "And it really cut deep. I was so angry, but I was caught off guard completely. He stormed out, and I just said to myself, 'Good, get out, stay out.' "

Tabitha said, "I meant what I just said in group. If you hadn't been there, I don't know how I could have stayed in the room. It was awful. But I did love the group members and how they came through. Betty, bless her, was probably trying to redeem all whites! But she was so caring. And everyone. It actually started some healing and, I think, brought us together. Amazing!"

Too tired to go on, they decided to stop for now. They scheduled a follow-up processing session for 2 days from then, deciding to focus on analyzing their group plan and how it might not have gone just as they had hoped. Coming back 2 days later to resume their processing, they were in a far different place psychologically and emotionally.

"Where, oh where, did we go wrong?" began Tabitha.

"Tabitha, don't you be so negative right away," chastised Chaunston. "After all, didn't the session end on a good note? Look, Doreen said it best, but the others seemed to be right there with her."

"Okay, okay, guilty as charged," said Tabitha. "But come on, look, stuff went wrong, right? Our changes didn't completely work."

"You mean, Anthony?" asked Chaunston.

"Yeah, he's certainly part of it, but I think we're through with what he did, at least for now. No, I mean more about how we're trying to focus the group more. The bigger picture here is what I think we need to stay focused on."

"Oh, if you mean we didn't reach perfection yet, yeah, we have some way to go," agreed Chaunston.

"I knew you'd see the light," Tabitha continued the friendly bantering. "Now let's settle down and see if we can figure out what we need to do to improve this group, okay?"

So they began to review the group from its planning stages some 12 weeks before. They reminded each other that the modifications approved for this group, and their potential spread to future groups of the center, were contingent on results.

"I'm aware of feeling extra pressure in this group because we are doing something different, one of a kind for our center. And the pilot-testing nature of it all adds to the pressure. How about you?" asked Chaunston.

"Oh, yeah, uh huh," Tabitha quickly responded. "And I'm wondering if we are going to have any way to provide the kind of data that would be useful. . . . You know that conference I attended that was so good? At one session on clinical outcomes in group therapy, they took a look at this kind of issue. I brought some of the handouts here." They began to look at and discuss the materials.

"These are very helpful, Tabitha!" said Chaunston. "We probably are not gathering enough data on our members before group, in looking at these forms. We really don't need any more surprises like Anthony's! Unless we do a group on racial attitudes or getting along with others who are different from us or something, which we might want to consider, actually. The MMPI is okay, but I really like the idea of getting information about them that is more tied to group and interpersonal things. This Emotions Profile Index seems as if it could be very helpful. And helping members to set goals through this Target Goals approach would be too. The Self-Report Symptom Inventory (SCL-90-R) here might be helpful to complement the MMPI-2. All these would give us more measures that we could then follow up on at the end."

"Yeah, and oh my, Chaunston, we have not been systematically gathering any kind of data ourselves, and we really need to. See here, we could complete the Target Goals form, too, and this Group Descriptive Data form seems easy to do, but it would summarize lots of important information. You know, in looking back, I think we've been overlooking some important procedures here, like assessment. I know we've wanted to keep things more personal and less formal and clinical in the center, and this has served us well with the Crossroads community, for sure. So bringing in more assessment would no doubt improve our documentation, but I hope it wouldn't get in the way either."

"That's a wonderful point," Chaunston said. "Me too. At any rate, it's too late for us to do any additional assessment of members now, but we could include the data form and maybe even the goals stuff, even though the group is half over."

"Yes, let's do that," said Tabitha. "Especially with the goals, if we build them into the group therapy."

"Yes, and that reminds me that an important part of all this is what will we do with the data. What's it for?" asked Chaunston. "Documentation and evaluation is one thing, and it's important, especially for our group right now. I think that if we could develop a preassessment package—we almost have it now—but then use it to help make selection and assignment decisions, that would be an advancement."

"That's very consistent with what was discussed in the conference, Chaunston. And beyond that, something we didn't get to for our group but talked about doing is to build the data into member preparation for the group."

Chaunston couldn't agree more. "Tabitha," he said forcefully, "this is still the biggest need we have, I think. It's to be able to match the kind of therapy group being provided with members suitable for that group's focus. That's what we are trying to do, at least in our group it is. And then to prepare the members before the first session for what to expect!"

"We had problems on both counts," said Tabitha.

"Absolutely. I think we're moving in the right direction, though, Tabitha. But yes, we had problems and probably still do, I agree. Anthony was a big one, of course—by the way, I will call him, just to follow up but not to get him back—and the unfortunate situation with Maxine. Look, we were concerned about dropouts when we started the group, and we have had two of seven already do that! Not good, but I think it's because our group's focus on substance abuse did not relate to their needs and problems. Looking back, we probably should not have let them in, really, and instead found some other better spot for them. These are the kinds of things we can try to fix in the future, don't you think?"

"I think so, yes," said Tabitha. "And the part about preparation of members for group. One of our continuing problems is that just about all of them still are uncertain about what to do in group, what it's for—"

Chaunston broke in. "Thanks for keeping that before us. Look, I just had an idea! If we use the goals form in the next session with them, that might give us a good chance to also address the group and what it can do and what they can do in the group to reach their goals."

"Great!" exclaimed Tabitha. "That's good, it seems to fit naturally and should help. Andre and the rest now seem much more energized to do something. But I'm not at all sure they know what. We need to help them clarify this. And then we should back this preparation up for future groups before Session 1: what the group is all about, what will happen, what their goals are, and that sort of thing. Actually, it's informed consent. Here's a handout from the conference that addresses the kinds of things we might be doing during preparation."

"Guess I should have gone to that conference with you," said Chaunston. "It seems to me that lots of what we are talking about here could be of benefit to the whole staff too. We might want to consider making a presentation to them on it during an upcoming staffing."

"Maybe, Chaunston. But let's hold off until we have at least this group under our belts and feel confident we have something of value to offer."

They concluded their processing session by focusing on themselves, at what was a deeper level.

"Back to Anthony's diatribe for a moment, okay?" asked Tabitha. "I'm black, you're black. There's nothing we can do to alter that, and nothing I would ever want to do. I'm proud to be an African American woman. Still, the hurt I felt from his words was deep. And I was so sad and scared, I thought that the group would fold and that I couldn't do anything to help it cause I was kind of incapacitated. Do you know what I mean?"

Chaunston knew because he was in the same place. No matter how secure one is about anything, including racial and ethnic identity, he thought, attacks at such core dimensions of one's life will have an impact and pose difficulty.

"All I can say is, thank God for the group. They carried me through, I'm not kidding. In fact, this group and what we are trying to do with it feels like just about the best kind of continuing education experience I've ever had," he said. "I'm aware of lots of learning happening, Tabitha. Maybe I've been stuck for too long, just doing what was always done with our groups. I'm feeling challenged to grow, to think about and do new things here. I'm grateful to you for assisting me with all this. Thank you."

"Oh, me too," said Tabitha. "You're so great to work with, Chaunston. You know what I'm finding? That I don't know nearly so much as I thought I did! I've got a long way to go to improve my leading and our groups. And I'm thinking that it's good to become aware of this so the changes can occur in me."

"Good," offered Chaunston. "As we continue to tighten up our therapy group, we'll be expanding ourselves, it sounds like. Not bad for some old timers, is it?" He laughed.

ANALYSIS

Follow the Best Practice Guidelines

The center's emphasis on community values associated with inclusion, diversity, heterogeneity, and informality significantly contributed to its positive reputation. Moreover, adoption of group-oriented services, consistent with the symbolic "circle," connected with compatible cultural themes of interdependence that generally characterized the main populations served in the center's catchment area. These approaches demonstrate how services can be designed to fit the ecological characteristics of a community, with a desirable emphasis on diversity.

Although the Crossroads Center had many factors going for it, it was becoming increasingly apparent to staff that the group program was in need of examination. High dropout rates and other signs of dissatisfaction were becoming more evident. Supporting the experimental trial of Chaunston and Tabitha's more focused therapy group on substance abuse showed the center's commitment to innovation. Further, it illustrated the importance of how innovation and evaluation are interrelated functions.

Moving in the direction of increased focus and precision is very consistent with the group psychotherapy literature and in keeping with the ideal of being responsive to emerging trends and changes in the field. Moreover, becoming more focused was responsive to a major short-coming in the center's group program. With the intention of mirroring important community values of diversity, the center had unwittingly ignored instituting important and necessary procedures and practices in its groups. Significant deficiencies existed in the areas of member selection, member preparation, matching member needs to appropriate groups, and assessment and evaluation.

Utilize Group Work Competencies

The coleaders were on target as they experimented with lending greater focus to their upcoming group. Here, they were trying to reduce one source of dissonance. What they failed to do was to match this more homogeneous group focus with members' presenting needs. This error in member selection helps to explain why Maxine and Anthony could not connect with the group, becoming dropouts. Moreover, the coleaders made no effort to prepare the members for the approaching group therapy experience. Consequently, members tended to flounder in the group, uncertain about how they were supposed to behave, what group participation could provide, and what they could seek to accomplish through the group.

Anthony's blatant racist attack on the group leaders and all African Americans was an unfortunate outcome of poor selection procedures being used but, more important, of how racism remains a potential factor to be contended with in all groups. This raw aggression was obvious, but frequently racism is more subtly expressed in groups by veiled comments, innuendoes, discounting, and other behaviors. Leaders need to develop their knowledge, attitudes, and skills to be able to constructively and openly address all "isms" (e.g., racism, ageism, sexism) in their groups.

In this case, the group easily could have been blown apart by the bomb that Anthony dropped. What saved the group were the caring responses of group members, which turned the ugly incident into what appeared to be a gain. This contribution by members shows the sometimes surprising strength of member resources in sustaining and deepening group life. Though frequently therapy group members may not have the resources to behave so helpfully, they should not be sold short. Within limits, leaders need to learn how to trust members and the group to be helpful, recognizing that members are often the most valuable resource of the group.

The leaders' recognition during processing that they could begin to address some problems within the present group also was a major step forward. Beginning to collect the goals data represents this movement. Incorporating evaluation data into group leading practice holds the potential to increase clarity, as well as to enable evaluation of change to occur.

For the long term, the leaders were able to identify what they could begin instituting for future groups, such as preparation procedures.

Moreover, their emerging awareness of the need for their own continuing learning was a major plus, demonstrating how deep processing can potentially influence lasting change.

QUESTIONS FOR REFLECTION AND DISCUSSION

1. Diversity is a value that is central to group work. The leaders determined in their situation, however, that too much diversity was present, to the extent that cohesion was compromised. Do you agree with them? Would you have taken a different approach? If so, what would it have been?

2. The leaders' attempt to focus the content of the group on substance abuse, while retaining demographic diversity, was not completely successful due to the admission of two members with different presenting problems than substance abuse. What alternatives might have Chaunston and Tabitha pursued instead of "mixing" the content? What about the role of assessment, of selection, of pregroup preparation? What are your thoughts about homogeneity versus heterogeneity? What might you have done if you were in the role of leader here?

3. Anthony's blatant racist attack on the leaders and other African Americans was repugnant and could have been a devastating blow to the group. If you had been in the coleaders' shoes, how do you imagine you would have been feeling? What might you have done?

4. Racism and other forms of discrimination are antithetical to group therapy practice, and openness to human diversity is strongly desired. Consider your thoughts, feelings, attitudes, values, and behavior with regard to diversity and group work. What do you find?

5. Group members played an important role in beginning to heal the wounds resulting from the racially motivated verbal attack. To what extent do you think group therapists can generally count on group members to be responsive and helpful in times of difficulty? Consider your response in relation to your working philosophy of group leadership.

CHAPTER 9

You Need to Trust the Process

BACKGROUND

The advent of managed care in mental health delivery has spawned many changes, including a heightened awareness of accountability. With regard to group therapy, two of the major responses to accountability have been the increased use of brief, short-term approaches in which the group therapist assumes an active role and the collection of outcome data to demonstrate effectiveness.

Both of these responses are consistent with values associated with cost-effectiveness, efficiency, and results. Some group therapists have found it necessary or attractive to provide more structure to their groups, to intervene more actively, and to focus on "bottom-line" outcomes (e.g., reduced symptomatology, fewer missed days of work) as well as on process.

Conversely, short-term, structured group therapy with a focus on outcomes and efficiency is not a direction that most group therapists would voluntarily choose to follow. For many, this orientation conflicts with their philosophical and strategic approach, which generally is more consistent with unstructured, process-oriented, and longer-term dimensions. As well, to the extent that these new directions are perceived as being imposed on them from external sources, such as managed care, clinic administration, or the marketplace in general, resistance by group therapists is a response to be expected. At the very least, it could easily be said that the pressure for instituting briefer, more active, outcome-oriented group therapy approaches is a subject that has generated much debate.

Saul Abrams had worked as a mental health therapist in private practice for 25 years. A substantial portion of his business always had been dedicated to group psychotherapy, his first love. His groups were long-term, with some members continuing for 3 years, and they were focused on an interpersonal-interactive change model emphasizing existential meaning.

Saul also consulted with the local branch of the mental health center on group therapy issues, and he was the primary source for training and supervision of their group therapists. Though the initiatives surrounding short-term groups affected Saul in his private practice, he experienced the biggest impact at the mental health center.

Saul's private practice clients were drawn largely from the business and professional world. Nearly all of these clients chose to remunerate services out of pocket, thus avoiding threats to confidentiality posed by third-party payers. They tended to be well off financially, were almost always self-referred, and selected Saul specifically because of his outstanding reputation as a group therapist and the unique focus of his group therapy. His therapy group practice, although somewhat more vulnerable due to the changes mentioned above, continued to thrive.

At the mental health center, however, a far different set of circumstances prevailed. Here the agency was becoming nearly completely dependent on insurance reimbursements and thus closely connected to the managed-care process. With this funding relationship, staff therapists were subject to the forces of short-term approaches that could be shown to be effective. These forces applied to the group therapy conducted in the center as well.

Saul found himself in a quandary of sorts. His professional orientation to group therapy, the very basis of his strong reputation, appeared to be in conflict with emerging mental health directions. Specifically, a mismatch was developing between the source of his expertise in group therapy and the kinds of groups that group therapists were expected to provide at the center. As he pondered this problem, in his worst moments Saul wondered if he was becoming an anachronism, out of touch with the times, having nothing of value anymore to offer younger group therapists. Alternately, his inherent optimism and the continued success of his private practice led him to naturally want to grapple with the issues and figure out a way how to use the abilities he knew he possessed in this new environment of accountability.

For years, the centerpiece of his group therapy training and supervision had been the staff supervision group. This group was composed of all staff conducting group therapy at the center, amounting in any one year to around eight staff. The purpose of the 2-hour, weekly supervision group, crafted by Saul with the first set of staff he had worked with

18 years ago, was "to develop a combined wisdom of what works in group therapy and of what it all means for us as group therapists."

The intent, if not the very existence, of this supervision group was now strained. Although the therapists to a person each retained a devotion and respect for Saul and his work, they had begun to express frustration about the tension they were feeling between his more open-ended model of group therapy and the brief, structured group therapy model that they were being urged by clinical administration to begin using.

This tension surfaced in the supervision group when Tom, a young therapist in his first year at the center, questioned the value of the interpersonal-interactive model. No one in the room had ever heard any staff member confront Dr. Abrams so directly.

"I'm sorry, Saul," he began, "but I'm just not sure the model we've been using—which is basically *your* model—can work anymore in the conditions we face! Maybe we need something closer to what gets rewarded, and that's brief, structured approaches!" He blurted out this thought in a flurry of emotion and then, realizing he had done so, felt embarrassed and turned a bright shade of red.

Nothing, though, could surprise Saul in a group. Though he fully recognized the unusual challenge that had just been put to him in this group, he had been preparing for it. He had seen this coming for awhile and, in a way, had been curious about just how it would manifest itself.

ACTION

Planning

The signs of discontent had been building. Saul had noticed especially the younger therapists, like Tom, pressing him some for group leader action methods. Two weeks before, there had been a discussion of the relevance of using the problem-solving method for organizing a group therapy session. Janet, who had been around now almost as long as Saul, had questioned the value of structuring sessions in that way, or any other way. A lively discussion had followed. Harold had taken up the matter of number of sessions, and Saul had asked him if he would research this matter and bring in his findings, which he did. It turned out that putting a limit on the number of group therapy sessions was gaining favor across the country and among members of their supervision group. Actually, Saul was not at all opposed to the idea as long as quality service could be continued.

The most significant issue that had sensitized Saul to the growing discontent of these therapy group leaders had emerged around the leader's role and function. They had all grown to appreciate the value Saul placed on the leader's serving as a culture builder who sought to facilitate interpersonal interaction and then to help members draw meaning from their here-and-now experience in the group. Attending to group process was a substantive part of this approach, as was allowing experiences and events to happen, rather than structuring their occurrence. Again, it was Tom who had raised some issues with this orientation, although he had done so quite obliquely. Saul remembered Tom asking, "Maybe we could think about being a bit more active as leaders?" in a way that was far more tentative than declarative.

Seeing and hearing these kind of issues being raised, Saul had taken time to think and plan his course of future action with the supervision group. He didn't like surprises and believed that "an ounce of prevention is worth a pound of cure." Reviewing the changes in the supervision group, which seemed to mirror those in the larger context of mental health care, Saul had concluded that there was much more underneath the questions being raised than had been expressed. What, exactly, he did not know, of course, but he imagined lots of feeling and maybe a real desire to explore behaving differently in their groups, perhaps to change completely to a briefer, more active leadership model.

Rather than resisting or defending against these mounting supervisee interests, Saul determined to be open to them, to invite them, to go "with the flow." After all, isn't this what any good group therapist would do?

Performing

So when Tom's direct question came, Saul was psychologically prepared. Calmly, he responded to Tom, hoping to engage him in an interaction.

"Tom, it looks like it took a lot for you to say that. I'm glad you did, thank you for it. It's okay, I'm fine with the question," he attempted to reassure Tom, whose redness was beginning to fade. "So let's talk about Tom's point. I think it's been coming for some time now, and maybe we'd better take a good look at it."

Saul's attitude about this issue was well received by everyone. His openness to discussion seemed to encourage openness in the members so that they were able to generate a lot of content and feelings.

"We feel caught in the middle, Saul," said Janet, a strong supporter of his approach. "How we have been trained and your work with us have helped us to be good at working with our therapy groups in one way. But all the pressure now is on working with them in a very different way. For one, I feel like my skills and value are being disregarded, and I don't know if I want to turn over a new leaf. No argument with being effective or with showing results. But group therapy is more than that—it's a human process that takes time to nurture and develop, it's not canned, and it can't be done in just a few sessions or done *to* people. As you've said time and time again, we work *with* people." Looking around, she ended, "Sorry for the speech, but that's where it is for me."

Many nodded in agreement. But the flip side was presented by Tom.

"Janet, you've put your finger on where my heart is with group therapy. Exactly. But let me try to speak from the other side for a minute. I've been trying to be more and more active in my groups, sort of as a test to see what it's like, and because that is what we are being nudged toward. Not from here, but from outside. Being more active, and shortening the number of sessions, and being very results oriented. Well, I've been trying the active part and—oh, yes—I've also included more testing in one group, too, to get at the results part some more than I have before. I used Horowitz's IIP, the Beck, and the SCL-90-R before the group, and I'll use it at the end, too. Remember, I talked about this assessment part some time ago. . . ."

Looking at Saul, Tom trailed off, as if he expected a response. Saul said nothing but nodded as if to say, "Okay, go on."

"So my little experiment with being more active, and more structuring, has been going on with this group since it began 3 weeks ago. And I feel like a rapid-fire gunner or something. I haven't brought it up here, I don't know why, maybe because I didn't think we were ready to talk about this kind of thing. Or maybe more likely because you would disapprove, Saul. But in any case, I need to talk about it now."

Here Saul chose to respond. Ignoring Tom's concern about disapproval, Saul wanted to get at Tom's actual performance, thinking that would be most helpful. "Would you like to take some time now to examine some of your work with this experiment, Tom?" Looking around at the others, Saul added, "And would this be okay with the rest of you?" All nodded.

"All right, Tom, you see, we could discuss and debate the politics of mental health service delivery now—maybe that would be a good idea or maybe we could do it at some other time. That doesn't seem to be what you're asking for right now. More like, 'Let's focus on my efforts to change.' Is that right?"

"Well, I'm really interested in both, Saul. But most important right now is how this group is going, yes."

"Fine, Tom. Go ahead, why don't you? Maybe with an example situation," suggested Saul.

"Good. Well, here's how this got started. I've been reading Spitz's book on group therapy and managed care, and some others, and a while ago I went to the Boston conference on brief approaches in mental health. I must confess, too, that some of this stuff makes good sense to me. The ideas for assessment came from the conference. I knew I couldn't change the number of sessions—the group had been set up already—so I decided to try to make some changes internally with my own style. Instead of sitting back, waiting more, allowing process to unfold—you know, our basic approach—I have begun to get involved and be active right from the start." Tom paused, took a deep breath, looked around the group, and admitted with emphasis on each word, "*It has not been without its difficulties!*"

As he listened, Saul wished Tom had presented his plan for experimenting with his leadership style before the group began. No doubt, this would have been more helpful to him and to everyone. Now it was happening midstream, and who knew what had happened, where things were? Saul considered, then rejected, taking this route for now.

"So you're in the midst of increased leader activity, testing it, noting how it's working, I suppose?"

"Yes, that's it. Plus, I don't know if I said this, I've been using many more structured exercises than ever before to focus and move the group forward," said Tom.

"So it's both more active and more structured, it sounds like," said Saul. "And you said it's been hard, or 'difficult,' I think, was the word you used. How about an example of what you've been doing so we can get a better handle on it?"

"Actually, Saul, I brought a tape with me, just in case. I can play the section I've marked that I think shows this very clearly—if this would fit?"

"Wonderful, even better," said Saul. And the other group members agreed, edging forward with anticipation.

"Okay, this is from the latest session, the third one, about halfway through. The group is one of our staples, on coping with depression.

There are six members—or there were, I'm not sure—that is what I want to look at. Anyway, here goes," said Tom, turning on the audiotape.

Tom was speaking. "I'm seeing quite a bit of silence today. I'm not sure what's going on, but maybe you're feeling stuck with something or just kind of low energy. Let's see if I can be helpful with this. What's on our agenda today is trying to specify our goals here. Let's come back to that by breaking into twos, dyads, that might help, instead of the whole group. Here, how about George and Myra, Susan and Carl, Bill and Millie. And then do this: Talk for about 10 minutes about your No. 1 goal for this group and how you might work on it. I'll keep track of the time, and then we'll come back to discuss this in our whole group. How does that sound?"

The tape gave forth the sound of silence for 10 seconds or so, interspersed with occasional coughing and a creaking chair. Tom broke it.

"Sometimes when I am asked to do something, I have trouble with that. I might not want to do it, or I don't like the idea, or something. Millie, how about you? Does any of that fit?"

Saul was wishing this were a videotape or the session could have been observed. So much is lost through only an audiotape! What are the members doing now, where are their eyes, what are their body movements? How does Tom look, what's he doing? He decided to ask Tom to pause the tape to get this information.

"Tom," interrupted Saul. "Could you pause the tape for a minute?"

"Sure," responded Tom as he pushed the pause button.

"A couple of things are running through my mind right now, Tom," said Saul. "One is, I wonder if anyone, you included, might have any comments at this point? The other is that I'm feeling a need to get a picture of what the group looks like nonverbally here—you know, body posture and so on. So much just doesn't get picked up with the audio."

"Yes, well, which first?" inquired Tom.

"Let's get the nonverbal stuff first, then we could field any comments," suggested Saul.

"All right, trying to think back," continued Tom. "Most of the time, they all are just looking away, or down. Millie seems a little energized, maybe agitated, or something; she rocks in her chair."

"How about when you speak to them?" asked Janet. "Is there any change?"

"No, I don't really think so," Tom replied. "Well, maybe with Millie, cause she seems to squirm more."

"Okay, thanks, Tom," said Saul. "If there isn't anything else about nonverbal things, maybe we could open for comments before moving on?" He looked to the others, opened his palm and reached out, inviting their comments.

"Yeah, I'm wondering, What happens with you, Tom, when they remain silent?" asked Janet. "It's interesting, because here you are, as you said, trying to become more active as a leader, but what you're getting is little or no participation from members, it seems from the tape here. Is that right?"

"Well, yeah, but you know in these kinds of groups, with people who are depressed and low energy, they usually aren't so active regardless. But as I think about it, and trying not to be too defensive here"—he laughed anxiously—"what you're saying does seem pretty accurate, Janet. At least my assumption was that my increased activity would get increased response. But that's clearly not working in this segment you're hearing, and it didn't throughout, I'll add," said Tom.

"All right," replied Janet. "Let's go on, if we can, cause I'm wondering about Millie. Not much for us to go on here, but is she reacting differently or more strongly than the others?"

"You're right on the money here, Janet!" Tom exclaimed. "I didn't really pick it up at the time, but—you know what—she later said, and it was painful for her, that she 'hated' my pushing and that she felt like leaving! I felt really bad about that."

Saul listened carefully to this interchange between Tom and Janet, trying to empathize with members of Tom's group, especially with Millie. Her word *pushing* Saul found compelling. Certainly, Tom didn't intend to push her or anyone, Saul was convinced. Rather, here was Tom trying on a new leadership style of becoming increasingly active and using more structure. Was it his more frequent involvement that Millie felt was the pushing? What buttons was Tom pushing in her? Saul wondered. Then he thought in another way of what might be going on here, where the group therapist can be considered as the instrument of change—that the therapist's needs and the member's needs can fit or conflict, and that when they conflict, problems can emerge.

"You know, Tom," he said, "I've been coming up with my own thoughts here about what might be going on. I know we really need to hear more of the taped segment, but given what we've gotten so far and our discussion of it, would you like to hear what I'm thinking?"

"Of course," Tom quickly replied.

"Okay, my frame here revolves around what you need and what they, especially Millie, need. An important need of yours in this group is to be helpful by becoming more active, by doing things that will help to move members and the group forward, and this level of activity is a different style for you. But maybe as you do this, your very activity is serving to shut down the members, to get in their way, even to drive them away. I'm hearing the possibility from Millie that your positive need to help feels to her like you are being 'pushy,' which she says she hates. Some members, maybe Millie, may feel like they are being engulfed."

"Boy, do you amaze me, Saul!" exclaimed Tom. "How do you come up with these thoughts so quickly? Let's slow it down some. What do you mean by 'engulfing?' "

"Yeah, I'm sorry, this may not fit. But let's see—what I mean is that by becoming more active you are also becoming more of a dominant figure in the group, more present and involved. You are providing lots of active interventions within the group, but you find members not responding actively in turn, contrary to what you expected. You continue to be active, but they seem to be moving away from you, rather than toward you."

Saul paused, looked around the group and saw signs of confirmation. He went on. "So I'm beginning to hypothesize that as you reach out, they retreat, almost abandoning you in the process. And what I said earlier about engulfment was that as you actively intervene, it may be misinterpreted as being pushy—that's what Millie termed it—and too much of that may lead her and perhaps some others to feel like you're not going to let them be, you're going to overrun them or engulf them. So they keep their distance. Underneath, you don't want to be abandoned, and they don't want to be engulfed. What do you think?"

"Hmm, I don't know, it's quite an interpretation, Saul, but it just seems a bit beyond what I can put together. It's deeper and more fear based, frankly, than I'm aware of, but maybe that's the point. I do feel like I'm pressing and they're not responding or, like Millie, kind of moving away from—" Tom paused in midsentence, thinking. "You know, what I'm beginning to come to here is that by being more active and using structure, like the pairings I used, I'm missing stuff that's important."

"Ah ha, could very well be!" Saul came back, and looked around the group of therapists. "Any thoughts?" he asked.

"Hard to say, for me," replied Linda, one of the other group therapists. "I wonder, Tom, do you have any other tape segments that could help here?"

"Well, let me see," said Tom, as he looked at his footage notes. "Maybe, let's see this one," as he fast-forwarded the tape.

"This is right about halfway through the session we have been discussing, and Bill is talking about problems he's having with getting out of bed, getting going for the day," reviewed Tom.

The tape resumed with Bill saying, "And then when I finally do get going, I'm just exhausted, all my energy is gone. It's deadly. I get to work late, and more often than not, lately, I bump into my boss, who I know just wonders what is going on with me!"

A brief gap in action occurred, and then Tom said, "Bill, let's do a role play of this with your boss. You be yourself, and who would like to play Bill's boss?" Someone was heard making a muffled, low sound that must have been an indication of volunteering. Tom said, "Good, George. Okay, Bill, can you give us a sense of how your boss looks and behaves in these situations when you bump into one another, to help George, here, to play him well."

Another silence. Tom said to Bill, "Just some description, you know, does he smile, say anything. . . ."

Here Linda interrupted, saying, "Saul, I have a thought. Can we stop the tape here?" Looking at Tom, she asked, "Tom?" Both nodded, and Tom stopped the tape.

Linda said, "Here's the idea I have, Tom. See what you think. Well, before that, let me ask if you could identify what your intent was by doing what you did—that is, setting up the role-play situation?"

"Well, again, I'm trying to be consistent with my approach here of using more active, structuring interventions, you know, the kinds of strategies that it seems to me are in line with the briefer groups that managed-care organizations are interested in. So yes, that's what I'm doing here," replied Tom.

"Okay," said Linda. "I'm assuming this is different from how you would ordinarily have responded to Bill, right?"

"Oh, yes, this is very different for me and probably for how any of us would usually work, I think. It's part of the experimenting I've been doing. When I think of what I might have done more typically, it would be more like letting that silence go some more, maybe asking if anyone else might have similar or different experiences, to try to get members talking to each other more," replied Tom.

"That's what I thought," responded Linda. "And it goes along with the idea I said earlier that I had. See, what I'm thinking is that instead of interjecting yourself into this with a structured activity like role playing, in this case, you could be more quiet here, or try linking, like you just said you might do otherwise."

As Tom weighed her suggestion, Saul followed up.

"Very interesting discussion," said Saul. "I think you're on to something important. The little clock on the wall says we're just about through for today. I have a suggestion, though. How about the two of you," he said, looking at Bill and Linda, "continuing to meet together for processing? Keep this going; it's very valuable."

Agreed. Tom and Linda set up a processing meeting to do just that.

Processing

As they began their processing meeting, Linda said to Tom, "You know, I had no idea Saul would ask us to get together about this, but then we do tend to use that approach sometimes, don't we? Guess it's part of Saul's notion that we are all helpers to each other. Anyway, I want to be sure you are all right with this, Tom."

"Really, I think it's a great idea, rather than waiting for our next supervision meeting. But thanks for checking this with me, Linda," said Tom.

"Okay, good. Where would you like to start?"

"Let's just see if we can get back to where we left off yesterday. I think you were suggesting something about being more quiet, or getting more connections—something like that, right?" replied Tom.

"Oh, yeah, that's where we were. Right. Well, what I think, I guess, is that you are working very hard at moving the group ahead, to kind of speed it up and make it more efficient, and that might come with some benefits but also with some deficits," offered Linda.

"Like what deficits are you thinking of?" asked Tom.

"Let me turn this around. Can you think of any?"

"Hmm, well, I certainly feel uncertain doing this, because it's not my usual way of working. That's one. I guess I do feel uncomfortable some with this more active style, like I'm pushing me, too. But I don't know about where Saul was going with the engulfment and, what, the abandonment discussion. That I can't really connect with."

"Okay, just stay with what makes sense to you right now, how's that?" suggested Linda.

"Good," said Tom, with some relief.

"What else, then, might be a deficit that you can see?" inquired Linda.

"Well, of course, if I'm trying to do something I am not sure of, then it could backfire, be ineffective, whatever. Those would be deficits, for sure," Tom replied.

"Okay, let's stick with those for a moment. Is any of that happening that you notice?" asked Linda.

"Yeah, I think so—Millie, for one, and some others seem to balk more than usual."

Linda was thinking about this. If not Saul's engulfment-abandonment idea, then what? Maybe Tom is simply getting in the way too much, being too intrusive, too controlling, she hypothesized.

"Maybe," she offered to Tom, "is it possible that you might be just in their way? That, in fact, you've succeeded in being more active and using more structure, but that by doing this you have gone too far, not leaving enough space for them? What do you make of that as a possibility?"

"Ai yi yi!" exclaimed Tom. "I just had an aha experience!" Sometimes awareness comes like a bolt of lightning, other times it moves more at the speed of a glacier. This one was the former times.

"Here's what I think is going on," said Tom, the words coming very fast now. "By being more centrally active, as you say, I've gone overboard. As a result of this, Linda," went on Tom, now with a smile of awareness spread across his face, "I've messed up. I haven't 'trusted the process'! And this, as we have always said around here, this capacity to 'trust the process,' is so essential to good group therapy. Man, how did I ever miss that!" exclaimed Tom, shaking his head in wonderment.

"It's obvious you've hit something that rings true for you, Tom. And that's a process to trust too! Great."

"Yes, yes, it does!" Tom quickly added. "I've got to get more balanced here, it's obvious to me."

"Tom, before jumping too quickly to action planning, would it be helpful to stay for a while with what meaning you are deriving from this series of events? You know, what Saul calls 'deep processing'?" asked Linda.

"Of course, sure. I'm probably being too active here too," Tom observed. "And I need to learn from the experience. You know, what I'm aware of is that in a rush to try out a more focused, active style that I think is desired by third-party payers, et cetera, I got too far away from *me* and what I do well. On the positive side, it is an experiment to be tested and evaluated. I don't think I've harmed anyone, at least not yet. But to trust the process is almost a mantra for me, for all of us here—that when the group is established properly, we can get out of the way some and let it take over more. I lost that perspective."

"But maybe there is something about becoming more active in your sessions that has merit, Tom," said Linda. "Do you think?"

"Well, if we can move to action steps now, yes, I think so. I think it's going to have to happen some anyway if we're going to survive in this marketplace. But I've got to be much more balanced about it. I've got to learn how to retain the focus on process and member involvement as I gradually become more active. I'm not sure how to do that, but it seems right," said Tom.

"Here's a thought," offered Linda. "I do think you're on to something important for yourself, and for all of us. Maybe you're like the 'leading edge' here for us. What if we go back to Saul and ask if we might be able to more systematically take a look at the issues you're raising and maybe use your present group as a test case for us all? Along with this notion of balance and of trusting the process that you've talked about today. What do you think, Tom?"

"That would be great, and it would feel very supportive to me too," agreed Tom. "What are the chances? What do you think Saul will say?"

"Saul is no dummy, that's for sure, as we all know. I think he realizes the need and will go for it," conjectured Linda. "Especially with this recognition that attending to process remains as critically important. 'Trust the process' was, after all, Saul's mantra, long before it was ours!"

ANALYSIS

Follow the Best Practice Guidelines

Group therapy, like all therapeutic approaches, has come under the influence of managed-care initiatives. Group leaders need to be aware of trends that affect the field, or that have the potential for doing so, and to anticipate changes needed. Though group therapy is now accepted as a valuable personal change vehicle, the pressure to make it even more efficient and effective is strong. Therefore, it behooves group therapists to familiarize themselves with the research literature and techniques associated with strategies that have become associated with efficiency and effectiveness.

Relative to efficiency, briefer, more structured approaches that involve the group therapist actively in the group represent an important trend. In terms of effectiveness, inclusion of assessment methods that can allow for determining more clearly if desired outcomes have been reached by members is another trend to explore. At the same time, group leaders must use their professional judgment and seriously consider their own values and skills in relation to making changes. It may be wise for group therapists to test out any new directions with a healthy amount of tentativeness and without summarily ejecting from their repertoire those beliefs, values, and practices that have played an important role in past success.

In the above case, both Saul and Tom are directly facing issues surrounding adapting their respective group therapy practices to brief, structured, action-oriented, and results-focused approaches. As the case moves to focus on Tom's experimentation with these factors in one of his groups, it becomes obvious that he has encountered some difficulties. As the nature of these difficulties is explored in more detail, and through his individual discussion with Linda, Tom surprises himself by redis-covering an old "chestnut" that he had temporarily lost in his quest to make his group therapy leading increasingly more efficient and effective: to "trust the process."

Utilize Group Work Competencies

Trusting the process, for many group therapists and other group workers, is a time-tested aphorism. Time and again, group therapists have learned that the biggest obstacle to successful group functioning is a tendency to step in and try to manipulate group and interpersonal process to produce some predetermined resolution instead of allowing the pro-cess to evolve naturally.

Of course, trusting the process can be misleading if the process itself is derived from a poorly laid group foundation and a group culture rife with dysfunction. However, if conditions, such as trust, confidentiality, and cohesion, have been developed effectively in the earlier stages of the group, then the group therapist can more reasonably select the strategy of trusting the process to help work through critical incidents. Members are then more likely to be able to assume increased responsibility for the group and themselves under the general guidance of the leader.

When a group therapist is moving in the direction of briefer, more structured groups in which the leader assumes an increasingly active role, reliance on group process is inadvertently compromised to some extent. In the case example, when Tom chose a role play to address Bill's depression, at least at that moment he was choosing a structured, active intervention over allowing group processes to evolve. This choice may have served to short-circuit the opportunity for members to be more naturally helpful to Bill. This is just one incident, and one cannot generalize from it very far. But if the general pattern is to use structure and active leader interventions, then it is safe to conclude that evolving process is being inhibited and that the capacity to "trust the process" is reduced.

The argument being advanced through the case is not to avoid moving in the directions being explored by Tom but rather to test them and to balance them with adequate attention to process. For it is group process that truly powers any therapy group. Group therapists must be careful to protect, sustain, and use it for therapeutic value.

QUESTIONS FOR REFLECTION AND DISCUSSION

1. The present and longer-term effects of managed care on group therapy are important to consider. As you ponder this issue, what thoughts do you have? What might the implications be for you?

2. Tom was experimenting with what for him were some new approaches to group therapy leadership: being more active, using more structure, concentrating more on member outcomes, and focusing the group more closely. What do you think of these directions for group therapy or for group counseling? How prepared might you be to implement these components in your own work?

3. How cognizant are you of assessment methods for group therapy? What is your thinking about including assessment measures such as those discussed in Chapter 1 of this book and referred to in this chapter? How do such measures relate to clinical observation and subjective forms of assessment?

4. Saul suggested that one explanatory factor for what was occurring in Tom's group might concern his needs as a therapist versus those of the members (i.e., the engulfment-abandonment discussion). Though this interpretation did not seem to "take" with Tom, what do you make of it in his situation? Or in yours?

5. In his efforts to become more active, structured, and oriented to results, Tom overlooked the dictum that serves as a guide for many

group leaders: "Trust the process." Under what conditions does "Trust the process" apply, do you think? Where might it not fit or, in fact, be inimical to success? What ideas do you have about including a process orientation with a content orientation in group therapy leadership?

6. Content and process need to assume a reasonable balance in a psychotherapy group. A continued focus on one without the other often is associated with negative results. What indicators would you use in determining a content-process balance? What could you do as a group leader to promote a content-process balance that works in your groups?

PART VI

Conclusion

CHAPTER 10

Learning From Our Mistakes Through Processing

In the foregoing eight chapters, you encountered examples of how group work leaders make mistakes but, with proper attention, can recover and move forward. Task group mistakes were made when a group work method was misapplied (Chapter 2) and culture was ignored (Chapter 3). Psychoeducation group mistakes occurred when content was overemphasized (Chapter 4) and a plan was not developed (Chapter 5). Counseling group mistakes happened when confidentiality was compromised (Chapter 6) and leader-member understandings were forgotten (Chapter 7). And psychotherapy group errors were made when procedural and diversity issues developed (Chapter 8) and process lost out to other priorities that were emerging as a response to managed care (Chapter 9).

Through these case examples you also have seen that failures can arise anywhere in the "3 P's" (planning, performing, and processing) of group work. Therefore, group leaders need to give each of these functions, and their interrelationship, adequate and consistent attention.

In this concluding chapter, I give more extensive attention to the third "P" of group work leadership, processing, which was introduced in Chapter 1. Processing is a reflective leadership function that leaders use between sessions to improve their understanding and functioning as group leaders. By so doing, they are far better able to convert mistakes into successes.

Though it is related, between-session processing should be distinguished from within-session processing, which, by definition, occurs during the performance of group leadership. As Jacobs, Harvill, and Masson (1994) defined within-session processing, it is concerned with group member thoughts, feelings, and ideas that result from group activity. Within-session processing is critically important to effective groups (Yalom, 1995), and it has received far too little attention (DeLucia-Waack, 1997) in the professional literature.

But now let us return to between-session processing, the focus of this chapter. Processing may occur between group leaders and their supervisor as coleaders meet for debriefing and planning, and/or it can be accomplished by a solo leader through his or her own independent analysis and reflection. All too frequently, however, processing is not incorporated into the regimen of group leaders at all, or it is done so quickly and incompletely. Failure to conduct processing, or to do it well, can lead to failures in group work leadership. As the saying goes, "The unexamined life is not worth living."

FAILURES, AND OUR RELUCTANCE TO INCLUDE PROCESSING

Failures, of and by themselves, are undesirable. However, what can turn failures into successful learning experiences that expand the range of available and appropriate group leader options is how the failures are approached.

If we as group leaders never or only rarely examine our work with an eye toward learning from it, then we will not open ourselves to learning and advancement. This statement is true equally for positive and negative group work experiences, for our successes as well as our failures.

If all is going well with our groups, we will be unable to identify the reasons for this happy state unless we take the time to examine them. Of course, this is frequently the last thing many of us choose to do with successes; we prefer just to keep on doing whatever seems to be working. When we are physically healthy, for example, we tend to give little attention to why this is the case. But in doing so, we miss gigantic learning opportunities.

We may be more likely to scrutinize failures, either of our own volition or because someone else demands it. When we are sick, the likelihood is greater to seek diagnoses and remedies for what is wrong. The same approach applies to group work. When a session "crashes," as when a plane crashes (though with much less devastating results, of course), group leaders may more readily try to understand why, or their supervisors may urge them to do so.

Being open to learning from our experiences as group leaders is fundamentally important. Maintaining this stance, however, is difficult for many group leaders.

Obstacles to Processing Failure (and Success) Experiences

There are a variety of reasons why group leaders may avoid examination of themselves and their work, thereby inhibiting a valuable growth opportunity. I offer five possible explanations below, each born out of my own observations and experience.

First, our society in general is fast paced, leaving rare time available for study and circumspection. This is a time-and-motion problem.

Second, Western culture tends to emphasize action and reaction, not analysis and reflection. In general, we are people who emphasize the doing of things, not the study of things. This problem is cultural and normative.

Third, in education, mental health, and human service settings, there is, as in business settings, a "bottom-line" focus on moving product and profitability. Group leaders are expected not only to benefit group members and/or group productivity but also, typically, to generate and document service units. Little time, therefore, is usually made available for group leaders to think critically about their groups or themselves as group leaders. This problem emerges from values and rewards in the workplace.

Fourth, self-examination can be risky. Some group leaders may find that such scrutiny places them in a vulnerable position that they would rather avoid.

Fifth, reflecting about group work practice is a skill set that needs to be learned, and relatively little attention is given to it in training programs. This problem revolves around skill deficits.

I will focus in this chapter on the fifth problem, deficits in training and in skills that serve to restrict or prevent the self-examination of group leadership. I will present and discuss a five-step method of processing that group leaders can use and educators can teach. Use of this method can help group leaders to become better informed, more self-aware, and increasingly effective.

PROCESSING AS A "FAILURE TRANSFORMER"

Processing is a leader function that fits within the line of inquiry associated with "reflective practice" (Schön, 1983), being a "reflective therapist" (Kottler & Blau, 1989), "action science" (Argyris, Putnam, & Smith, 1987), "action research" (Lewin, 1951), "social constructionism" (Gergen, 1985; Monk, Drewery, & Winslade, 1997), and related conceptions. Though these conceptions vary in terms of emphasis and complexity, they share placing importance on connections between doing and thinking about doing, or, as Schön (1983) put it, reflecting-in-action. That is, actions are critically analyzed by the actor, resulting in learning and meaning that the actor uses to intentionally inform and guide subsequent action.

Processing involves group leaders in applying the concepts summarized above. Group leaders examine their groups and themselves, learn from doing this, and then apply what they have learned in a planned way. Group work leadership informed and guided by reflection is critically important to processing, and it makes group leaders better able to turn apparent failures into successes.

Processing can stimulate learning and growth for group leaders, thereby expanding their awareness and potential. In a very real sense, processing can transform failure. As Kottler and Blau (1989) observed:

> We have come to realize that failure is not only an inevitable component of therapeutic practice, but a potentially useful one in the learning and growth it can stimulate. . . . We have seen that failure need not be a diminishing experience. Indeed, we can regard it as an opportunity for expanding our repertoire of options. (p. 149)

Levels of Processing: Pragmatic and Deep

As you may recall from Chapter 1, I identified two levels of processing, pragmatic and deep. These levels are both important and complementary.

In *pragmatic processing,* group leaders attempt to objectively, accurately, and concretely describe, without interpretation or manipulation of any kind (i.e., to "transpose"), all observations they made of events and experiences that occurred in the group session. Pragmatic processing is essential for identifying the specifics of what happened in a group session, giving consideration to participation levels, patterns of involvement, content addressed, leader involvement, and similar "objective" matters. It is my experience that when processing is engaged in by group leaders, it tends to stay largely at the level of pragmatic processing.

Deep processing is an extension of pragmatic processing. It includes Steps 2 through 5 of the processing function, to be discussed in more detail below. In deep processing, leaders reflect on concrete, objective, descriptive data produced through pragmatic processing in relation to their subjective experience. They actively consider the implications of events, search for learning and meaning, and give attention to the relationship between what occurred and their thoughts, feelings, and values. In deep processing, the leaders attempt to apply learning and created meaning to their immediate and longer-term professional practice. Although it is possible to engage in processing at the pragmatic or deep level, a complete processing includes both levels.

THE FIVE STEPS OF PROCESSING

How can group leaders engage in processing? They can be guided by the following five cyclical steps.

Step 1 is to *transpose,* or closely observe and describe without interpretation, what occurred during a group session. Transposing involves pragmatic processing. Examples include: "Describe exactly what happened in the session," "Describe concretely any patterns of interaction among members in the group," and "Describe dominant behaviors demonstrated during the session by members."

Step 2 is to *reflect* on, and sometimes confront, what was done, involving one's thoughts, awareness, sensations, feelings, and values. Reflecting is the first step of deep processing. Examples include: "Describe your thought pattern as you considered intervention choices," "Describe how you were feeling as the same members continued to interact," and "What were you aware of during the long silences of the two members that you just indicated?"

Step 3 is to *discover* learning and created meaning from reflection by linking with conceptual knowledge and drawing out insights. Discovering is the second step of deep processing. Examples include: "I realize now that I was missing a lot of important data from the group as I thought about interventions," "I was becoming very anxious about the same folks talking to each other and wondering about what my role should be," and

"I was feeling bad for the silent members, wanting to reach out and get them involved and talking—maybe too much so."

Step 4 is to *apply* intentionally what was derived and created by designing action strategies to be tried and tested. Applying is the third step of deep processing. Examples include: "I need to wait and gather more information before forming interventions," "Next time I might look for the anxiety and welcome it, rather than resist it," and "Feeling bad for members is not what they need; maybe I will try speaking to them about my concerns."

Step 5 is to *evolve* personal principles of group leadership (e.g., see Conyne, 1997), that have longer-term significance and sustaining power for oneself as a group leader. Evolving is the last step of deep processing. Examples include: "Don't rush in with actions until the data are accounted for," "Trust your own internal reactions and incorporate them into your functioning as a leader," and "All things considered, when in doubt, ask."

In practice, the steps of processing may not be followed in the exact sequence above and should not be approached in a lockstep manner. Rather, as with any method of learning and change, one has to apply its steps sensitively and naturally, providing a good fit with the processing situation. It is important, as well, to recognize that the five steps of processing are cyclical and interdependent. Each one influences and is influenced by the others.

Reviewing an Example of How Processing Was Done

Let us take a look at how processing was used in one of the chapters you have read (Chapter 4). Now that the five steps of processing have been presented, a review of this case can provide a sense of how processing can be accomplished.

Context. In Chapter 4 (you may find a quick review of Chapter 4 useful at this point), you will recall that Donna became quite focused on delivering her plan, so much so that she missed the "driving force" of group process. This experience strongly affected her, as manifested by her recurring nightmare. She was at a loss, both in terms of what to do to salvage her group and also personally.

Openness to Exploration. Donna had the good sense to approach her supervisor, Tom, with an openness to learning. This, of course, is a key to any effective supervisory relationship, and it is a central feature of effective processing too.

Processing Step 1: Transposing. As they begin their session, Tom asks Donna to describe what happened. He reaches for behaviors and concrete indications. He asks her questions such as "Now what did they do when they were there?" and "Okay, good. Let's talk about you in the group, can we, Donna? Tell me more about what you were doing and feeling there." Here Tom is orienting their discussion to Step 1 of the processing model, transposing. As you have seen, transposing is the equivalent of pragmatic processing. Donna is asked to enumerate and objectively describe events as they happened.

Processing Step 2: Reflecting. After getting some descriptive information before them in this way, Donna quickly moves to her feelings. Tom notices that Donna is tied affectively to what happened. She quickly admits to feeling like a failure, which is a most difficult admission to make to your supervisor. He allows her to move to Step 2, reflection, as she describes feelings, thoughts, and sensations that accompanied her incessant talking at the members. She says, "But I had the strange sensation of standing off from myself, looking at what was going on, knowing that it was just not going well. Boy, that was frustrating—and I felt like a failure." Tom later asks Donna directly for her feelings and then even guides her to examine a particular frame for understanding. He asks her, "Can you remember how you were feeling during those moments? Anything about self-talk at those points?"

Processing Step 3: Discovering Learning and Creating Meaning. This question stimulates Donna to move from Step 2 (reflection) to Step 3 (discovering learning, creating meaning) of the processing model. Here she makes a startling connection between the lack of control she felt during the session and a similar sensation she experienced during her nightmare of the sinking ship. She reveals, "Tom, I think I was trying to save the group, as stupid as that sounds now! And I worked so hard at it, took all of this on myself as the leader, that I trapped myself into allowing no room for members to participate." Donna has derived a significant insight from this apparent failure, which Tom acknowledges: "Wow, that really seems like a significant insight, Donna. You have put this together very quickly. How does it seem to you?" This leads Donna to an even deeper meaning: "I've been able here to identify deeper reasons for why I just kept filling the air. And I'm thinking that with this awareness now, that I'm freed up from running the show, doing everything."

Processing Step 4: Applying. Donna naturally directs movement to application by asking herself, and Tom, aloud: "Now the question is, how do I do that? And how can I begin doing it this very next session?" This lengthy discussion produces suggestions by Tom and by Donna. For example, she realizes that she will need to start including opportunities for members to process the group and how it was going. And Tom helps her to see how she could "build a bridge" between the first and second sessions. Through the application step of processing, Donna has been able to identify specific actions she can take to avert failure.

Processing Step 5: Evolving Sustaining Principles. Processing has allowed Donna to gain direction for the immediate group session that she is facing. Significantly, it has also helped her formulate a principle that holds larger, longer-term significance. This principle is twofold: the importance of the driving force of group process in relation to her interfering need for control. She realizes, "What I did was to miss the driving force of the group just about entirely by focusing on me and my need to control or to make things happen. I'll work on myself. It's me more than anything else."

Donna can use this principle to guide future group work leadership, not just the next session of the current group. In doing so, she will be in a good position to prevent failures from occurring.

YOUR CHANCE TO USE PROCESSING: CASE APPLICATION

Presented below is an abbreviated group work case example that is awaiting your processing. It is arranged in keeping with the format of previous chapters, although it is not nearly as long. As you are reading it, try to begin applying in your mind the five steps of processing: (a) transposing, (b) reflecting, (c) discovering, (d) applying, and (e) evolving. Getting practice with using the processing steps will help you to understand better what is going well in your groups and enable you to prevent, or recover from, failures.

Background

Sam and Fran are counseling practicum students who are leading their first group. This is a psychoeducation group focusing on social skills for adolescents. It is being conducted at the Redfield High School. The group consists of three girls and five boys, all of whom are sophomores. One of the members, William, is African American, and the other members, and the coleaders, are white. This is the ninth of 10 group sessions.

Planning. In their planning for this group, Fran and Sam sought to create a tightly woven series of sessions that were developmentally sequenced. Within each session they had carefully designed activities that allowed for the presentation of information about selected social skills, practice of these skills, and feedback.

Performing. The previous eight sessions had been progressing pretty much according to plan. There had been a noticeable absence of conflict, and all members but William had been participating actively. The coleaders had been able to work well together, they thought, and they believed the group was a success.

Processing. Sam and Fran had been able to meet for processing every week but the one, when Fran had been ill. In their supervision group, they also occasionally got time to present their group, but not in any detail at all. When they met with Dr. Arnold, the faculty supervisor, they received some help, but groups were not really his area of expertise. On site, they had had good discussions with their supervisor about how the group was going. All parties seemed to agree that it was proceeding very well and that the group leaders were doing a fine job. William's lowered level of involvement never became a focus of discussion in any processing session, although from time to time both leaders wondered independently about it.

Performing: The Ninth Session

Fran and Sam were planning to begin wrapping up the group experience during this next-to-last session. They intended to begin helping members to focus intently on what they had learned during the experience and how they would apply these insights. Then, in the upcoming tenth and final session, they had planned to help the members to say goodbye, along with having a brief closing exercise.

Were they ever caught off guard! After the next-to-last member confirmed the feelings of all previous members by talking about her satisfaction with the group experience, it was William's turn. William spoke loudly, gesturing broadly, and he seemed disturbed or angry as he began. This was a surprise because, of all the members, he had been the most quiet and reserved.

"I'd just like to say," he said, looking directly at the leaders, "that *that's* not the way it was for me in here! After awhile I took this whole thing as a kind of game. After the first two meetings, and when nobody had asked me anything at all or even seemed interested, I mean. And remember when I said during the first meeting that I might feel out of place here, being the only black person? Remember what you all did?" he challengingly asked. He paused, as if to decide whether he wanted to go ahead or stop. "Well, no one said anything to me, just let it go! I don't even know if I should be saying any of this, but I'm just so fed up. I kept coming back, hoping something would change. But this group is like all the other ones where there aren't any black folks but me and it's like I'm just—just invisible or something!"

Sam and Fran were as taken aback as all the other members. They felt as if they'd been hit by a meteor from outer space, totally unexpected but packing a terrific wallop just the same. This wasn't in the plan, and they felt completely unprepared to cope with it. But it became clear to both of them that they must have missed something big with William. Had they ignored him because of his race? What a horrible thought that was, if true.

Fran replied. "William, I am so sorry if you felt that I—and the others in the group, if I can speak for them—somehow discounted you! I don't know what to say," she concluded, running out of ideas.

Sam followed up. "Gee, William, you've caught me by surprise. I really just thought that you preferred to be more quiet. I didn't try in any way to look over you or ignore you."

"Well, that's kind of funny," said William, "cause I remember your asking Sue," he said, glancing her way, "if she wanted to say something on two or maybe three different times in here! And she wasn't the only one either. But you never asked me. Is it because I'm black?"

Pow! What a direct confrontation. The room fell silent, but filled with thwarted energy and a lot of anxiety.

After what seemed to be an eternity, Sam replied to William. "Honestly, I don't think so, William. I think I misread the situation. But I'm going to look at this, think about it. It's something I am being challenged by in this group. Can we come back to this next week as we bring the group to a close? And William, I'm glad you said what you did, even though it doesn't feel real good to me right now."

Your Turn to Process

Imagine that you are an expert in group work who is well versed in the five steps of the processing model. Fran and Sam have sought you to consult about the situation they just faced in their ninth session. How would you assist them in working through the processing steps of transposing, reflecting, discovering, applying, and evolving?

Can you envision how progressing through these steps could help these coleaders turn their mistakes into possible positive movement? How might that occur? What questions associated with the five steps of processing might you ask them? What have you learned as you applied the five steps of processing to this case?

CONCLUSION

I worried as I wrote this book on mistakes and failures in group work that it might be too gloomy and disquieting to read. I hope it did not turn out that way.

Now that you are at the end of it, I also hope that you found the incidents presented to be stimulating and that you could connect with them. Moreover, I am optimistic that the primary message of this book was made clear: that by exercising proper planning, performing, and processing functions and by incorporating other best practices in group work, group failures can be prevented and sometimes rescued. Failures can be turned to successes.

I also hope that the book raised your awareness and understanding of the four types of group work (task, psychoeducation, counseling, and psychotherapy) that well-trained counselors and other helpers may use to improve personal and/or organizational functioning. It is important for the broad potential of group work to be implemented in a society that faces so many challenges. Group work is a powerful interpersonal vehicle that is particularly well suited for educating, healing, and changing these problems.

Group leaders need to engage in far more processing, especially deep processing, than is typically done. And of course, processing needs to be included in the group work curricula of training programs. Simply put, the emphasis on doing in group work leadership must be expanded and informed by reflecting about doing. Otherwise, the work of group leaders may rest unexamined as mistakes continue to mount.

I want to challenge you to actively explore the five steps of processing in your group work leadership. Find a way to set aside time, or build it into ongoing opportunities, to engage in transposing, reflecting, discovering, applying, and evolving. Place primary focus on the steps involving deep processing (reflect, discover, apply, and evolve), but include all steps. You will find that incorporating processing regularly into your work as a group leader will yield large dividends in your practice and for you personally.

Appendix
ASGW Best Practice Guidelines

Association for Specialists in Group Work
Best Practice Guidelines

Approved by the Executive Board March 29, 1998
Prepared by Lynn Rapin and Linda Keel,
ASGW Ethics Committee Co-Chairs

The Association for Specialists in Group Work (ASGW) is a division of the American Counseling Association whose members are interested in and specialize in group work. We value the creation of community; service to our members, clients, and the profession; and value leadership as a process to facilitate the growth and development of individuals and groups.

The Association for Specialists in Group Work recognizes the commitment of its members to the Code of Ethics and Standards of Practice (as revised in 1995) of its parent organization, the American Counseling Association, and nothing in this document shall be construed to supplant that code. These Best Practice Guidelines are intended to clarify the application of the ACA Code of Ethics and Standards of Practice to the field of group work by defining Group Workers' responsibility and scope of practice involving those activities, strategies and interventions that are consistent and current with effective and appropriate professional ethical and community standards. ASGW views ethical process as being integral to group work and views Group Workers as ethical agents. Group Workers, by their very nature in being responsible and responsive to their

173

group members, necessarily embrace a certain potential for ethical vulnerability. It is incumbent upon Group Workers to give considerable attention to the intent and context of their actions because the attempts of Group Workers to influence human behavior through group work always have ethical implications. These Best Practice Guidelines address Group Workers' responsibilities in planning, performing and processing groups.

SECTION A: BEST PRACTICE IN PLANNING

A.1. Professional Context and Regulatory Requirements

Group Workers actively know, understand, and apply the ACA Code of Ethics and Standards of Best Practice, the ASGW Professional Standards for the Training of Group Workers, these ASGW Best Practice Guidelines, the ASGW diversity competencies, the ACA Multicultural Guidelines, relevant state laws, accreditation requirements, relevant National Board for Certified Counselors Codes and Standards, their organization's standards, and insurance requirements impacting the practice of group work.

A.2. Scope of Practice and Conceptual Framework

Group Workers define the scope of practice related to the core and specialization competencies defined in the ASGW Training Standards. Group Workers are aware of personal strengths and weaknesses in leading groups. Group Workers develop and are able to articulate a general conceptual framework to guide practice and a rationale for use of techniques that are to be used. Group Workers limit their practice to those areas for which they meet the training criteria established by the ASGW Training Standards.

A.3. Assessment

a. *Assessment of self.* Group Workers actively assess their knowledge and skills related to the specific group(s) offered. Group Workers assess their values, beliefs, and theoretical orientation and how these impact upon the group, particularly when working with a diverse and multicultural population.

b. *Ecological assessment.* Group Workers assess community needs, agency or organization resources, sponsoring organization mission, staff competency, attitudes regarding group work, professional training levels of potential group leaders regarding group work, client attitudes regarding group work, and multicultural and diversity considerations. Group Workers use this information as the basis for making decisions related to their group practice, or to the implementation of groups for which they have supervisory, evaluation, or oversight responsibilities.

A.4. Program Development and Evaluation

a. *Group Workers identify the type(s) of group(s) to be offered and how they relate to community needs.*

b. *Group Workers concisely state in writing the purpose and goals of the group.* Group Workers also identify the role of the group members in influencing or determining the group goals.

c. *Group Workers set fees consistent with the organization's fee schedule, taking into consideration the financial status and locality of prospective group members.*

· d. *Group Workers choose techniques and a leadership style appropriate to the type(s) of group(s) being offered.*

e. *Group Workers have an evaluation plan consistent with regulatory, organization, and insurance requirements, where appropriate.*

f. *Group Workers take into consideration current professional guidelines when using technology, including but not limited to Internet communication.*

A.5. Resources

Group Workers coordinate resources related to the kind of group(s) and group activities to be provided, such as adequate funding; the appropriateness and availability of a trained co-leader; space and privacy requirements for the type(s) of group(s) being offered; marketing and recruiting; and appropriate collaboration with other community agencies and organizations.

A.6. Professional Disclosure Statement

Group Workers have a professional disclosure statement which includes information on confidentiality and exceptions to confidentiality; theoretical orientation; the nature, purpose(s), and goals of the group;

the group services that can be provided; the role and responsibility of group members and leaders; Group Workers' qualifications to conduct the specific group(s); specific licenses, certifications, and professional affiliations; and address of licensing/credentialing body.

A.7. Group and Member Preparation

a. *Group Workers screen prospective group members if appropriate to the type of group being offered.* When selection of group members is appropriate, Group Workers identify group members whose needs and goals are compatible with the goals of the group.

b. *Group Workers facilitate informed consent.* Group Workers provide in oral and written form to prospective members (when appropriate to group type) the professional disclosure statement; group purpose and goals; group participation expectations, including voluntary and involuntary membership; role expectations of members and leader(s); policies related to entering and exiting the group; policies governing substance use; policies and procedures governing mandated groups (where relevant); documentation requirements; disclosure of information to others; implications of out-of-group contact or involvement among members; procedures for consultation between group leader(s) and group member(s); fees and time parameters; and potential impacts of group participation.

c. *Group Workers obtain the appropriate consent forms for work with minors and other dependent group members.*

d. *Group Workers define confidentiality and its limits (for example, legal and ethical exceptions and expectations; waivers implicit with treatment plans, documentation, and insurance usage).* Group Workers have the responsibility to inform all group participants of the need for confidentiality and potential consequences of breaching confidentiality and to state that legal privilege does not apply to group discussions (unless provided by state statute).

A.8. Professional Development

Group Workers recognize that professional growth is a continuous, ongoing, developmental process throughout their career.

a. *Group Workers remain current and increase knowledge and skill competencies through activities such as continuing education, profes-*

sional supervision, and participation in personal and professional development activities.

b. *Group Workers seek consultation and/or supervision regarding ethical concerns that interfere with effective functioning as a group leader.* Supervisors have the responsibility to keep abreast of consultation, group theory, and process and to adhere to related ethical guidelines.

c. *Group Workers seek appropriate professional assistance for their own personal problems or conflicts that are likely to impair their professional judgement or work performance.*

d. *Group Workers seek consultation and supervision to ensure appropriate practice whenever working with a group for which all knowledge and skill competencies have not been achieved.*

e. *Group Workers keep abreast of group research and development.*

A.9. Trends and Technological Changes

Group Workers are aware of and responsive to technological changes as they affect society and the profession. These include but are not limited to changes in mental health delivery systems; legislative and insurance industry reforms; shifting population demographics and client needs; and technological advances in Internet and other communication and delivery systems. Group Workers adhere to ethical guidelines related to the use of developing technologies.

SECTION B: BEST PRACTICE IN PERFORMING

B.1. Self Knowledge

Group Workers are aware of and monitor their strengths and weaknesses and the effects these have on group members.

B.2. Group Competencies

Group Workers have a basic knowledge of groups and the principles of group dynamics and are able to perform the core group competencies, as described in the ASGW Professional Standards for the Training of Group Workers. Additionally, Group Workers have adequate understanding and skill in any group specialty area chosen for practice (psychotherapy, counseling, task, psychoeducation, as described in the ASGW Training Standards).

B.3. Group Plan Adaptation

a. *Group Workers apply and modify knowledge, skills, and techniques appropriate to group type and stage and to the unique needs of various cultural and ethnic groups.*

b. *Group Workers monitor the group's progress toward the group goals and plan.*

c. *Group Workers clearly define and maintain ethical, professional, and social relationship boundaries with group members as appropriate to their role in the organization and the type of group being offered.*

B.4. Therapeutic Conditions and Dynamics

Group Workers understand and are able to implement appropriate models of group development, process observation, and therapeutic conditions.

B.5. Meaning

Group Workers assist members in generating meaning from the group experience.

B.6. Collaboration

Group Workers assist members in developing individual goals and respect group members as co-equal partners in the group experience.

B.7. Evaluation

Group Workers include evaluation (both formal and informal) between sessions and at the conclusion of the group.

B.8. Diversity

Group Workers practice with broad sensitivity to client differences, including but not limited to ethnic, gender, religious, sexual, psychological maturity, economic class, family history, physical characteristics or limitations, and geographic location. Group Workers continuously seek information regarding the cultural issues of the diverse population with whom they are working both by interaction with participants and from using outside resources.

B.9. Ethical Surveillance

Group Workers employ an appropriate ethical decision making model in responding to ethical challenges and issues and in determining courses of action and behavior for self and group members. In addition, Group Workers employ applicable standards as promulgated by ACA, ASGW, or other appropriate professional organizations.

SECTION C: BEST PRACTICE IN GROUP PROCESSING

C.1. Processing Schedule

Group Workers process the workings of the group with themselves, group members, supervisors, or other colleagues, as appropriate. This may include assessing progress on group and member goals, leader behaviors and techniques, group dynamics, and interventions and developing understanding and acceptance of meaning. Processing may occur both within sessions and before and after each session, at time of termination, and at later follow-up, as appropriate.

C.2. Reflective Practice

Group Workers attend to opportunities to synthesize theory and practice and to incorporate learning outcomes into ongoing groups. Group Workers attend to session dynamics of members and their interactions and also attend to the relationship between session dynamics and leader values, cognition, and affect.

C.3. Evaluation and Follow-Up

a. *Group Workers evaluate process and outcomes.* Results are used for ongoing program planning, improvement, and revisions of current group and/or to contribute to professional research literature. Group Workers follow all applicable policies and standards in using group material for research and reports.

b. *Group Workers conduct follow-up contact with group members, as appropriate, to assess outcomes or when requested by a group member(s).*

C.4. Consultation and Training With Other Organizations

Group Workers provide consultation and training to organizations in and out of their setting, when appropriate. Group Workers seek out consultation as needed with competent professional persons knowledgeable about group work.

References

American Counseling Association. (1995). *Code of ethics and standards of practice.* Alexandria, VA: Author.

American Group Psychotherapy Association. (1995). *A consumer's guide to group psychotherapy* [Brochure]. New York: Author.

American Professional Credentialing Services. (1996). *Outcome Questionnaire.* Stevenson, MD: Author.

Argyris, C., Putnam, R., & Smith, D. M. (1987). *Action science: Concepts, methods, and skills for research and intervention.* San Francisco: Jossey-Bass.

Association for Specialists in Group Work. (1989). *Ethical guidelines for group counselors.* Alexandria, VA: Author.

Association for Specialists in Group Work. (1991). *Professional standards for the training of group workers.* Alexandria, VA: Author.

Association for Specialists in Group Work. (1998). *Association for Specialists in Group Work best practice guidelines.* Alexandria, VA: Author.

Attkisson, C. (1984). *Client Satisfaction Questionnaire.* San Francisco: Author.

Battle, C., Imber, S., Hoehn-Saric, R., Stone, A., Nash, E., & Frank, J. (1966). Target complaints as criteria of improvement. *American Journal of Psychotherapy, 20,* 184-192.

Bentz, V. M. (1992). Deep learning groups: Combining emotional and intellectual learning. *Clinical Sociology Review, 10,* 71-89.

Bloom, B. S., Engelhart, M., Furst, E. J., Hill, W. H., & Krathwohl, D. (1956). *Taxonomy of educational objectives: The classification of educational goals.* New York: McKay.

Brothers, P. (1997, June 1). Dilbert creator thrives on failure. *Cincinnati Enquirer,* pp. 13-14.

Brown, B. M. (1997). Psychoeducation group work. *Counseling and Human Development, 29,* 1-14.

Burlingame, G., & McCollam, P. (Eds.). (1998, Winter). Assessing change in your clients [Special issue]. *Group Solution.*

Canfield, J., & Hanscn, M. V. (1993). *Chicken soup for the soul: Stories to open the heart and rekindle the spirit.* Deerfield Beach, FL: Health Communications.

Conyne, R. K. (Ed.). (1985). *The group workers' handbook: Varieties of group experience.* Springfield, IL: Charles C Thomas.

Conyne, R. K. (1989). *How personal growth and task groups work.* Newbury Park, CA: Sage.

Conyne, R. K. (1997). Group work ideas I have made aphoristic (for me). *Journal for Specialists in Group Work, 22,* 149-156.

Conyne, R. K., Rapin, L. S., & Rand, J. (1997). A model for leading task groups. In H. Forester-Miller & J. Kottler (Eds.), *Issues and challenges for group practitioners* (pp. 117-131). Denver, CO: Love.

Conyne, R. K., Smith, J., & Wathen, S. (1997, October). *Co-leader and supervisor processing of group phenomena.* Paper presented at the annual meeting of the North Central Association for Counselor Education and Supervision, St. Louis, MO.

Conyne, R. K., & Wilson, F. R. (1998). Toward a standards-based classification of group work offerings. *Journal for Specialists in Group Work, 23,* 177-184.

Conyne, R. K., Wilson, F. R., & Ward, D. E. (1997). *Comprehensive group work: What it means and how to teach it.* Alexandria, VA: American Counseling Association.

Corey, G. (1995). *Theory and practice of group counseling* (4th ed.). Pacific Grove, CA: Brooks/Cole.

Corey, G., & Corey, M. S. (1997). *Groups: Process and practice* (5th ed.). Pacific Grove, CA: Brooks/Cole.

Corey, G., Corey, M. S., Callanan, P. J., & Russell, J. M. (1992). *Group techniques* (2nd ed.). Pacific Grove, CA: Brooks/Cole.

Craik, F. I. M., & Lockhart, R. S. (1972). Levels of processing: A framework for memory research. *Journal of Verbal Learning and Verbal Behavior, 11,* 671-684.

Cummings, N. A. (1995). Impact of managed care on employment and training: A primer for survival. *Professional Psychology: Research and Practice, 26*(1), 10-15.

D'Andrea, M., & Daniels, J. (1997). RESPECTFUL counseling: A new way of thinking about diversity counseling. *Counseling Today, 40,* 30-31, 34.

DeLucia-Waack, J. (1997). Editorial: The importance of processing activities, exercises, and events to group work practitioners. *Journal for Specialists in Group Work, 22,* 82-84.

DeLucia-Waack, J. L. (1998). Measuring the effectiveness of group work: A review and analysis of process and outcome measures. *Journal for Specialists in Group Work, 22,* 277-293.

Derogatis, L. (1975). *Self-Report Symptom Self-Inventory (SCL90-R)*. Baltimore: Clinical Psychometric Research.

Dies, R. R. (Ed.). (1978). Therapy and encounter group research: Issues and answers [Special issue]. *Small Group Behavior, 9*(2).

Dolan, J. D. (1998). Pool: A love story. *Esquire, 129*(2), 84-89.

Ettin, M., Heiman, M., & Kopel, S. (1988). Group building: Developing protocols for psychoeducational groups. *Group, 12*, 205-225.

Forester-Miller, H., & Davis, T. (1995). *A practitioner's guide to ethical decision making*. Alexandria, VA: American Counseling Association.

Gazda, G. (1989). *Group counseling: A developmental approach* (4th ed.). Boston: Allyn & Bacon.

Gergen, K. (1985). Social constructionist theory: Context and implications. In K. Gergen & K. Davis (Eds.), *The social construction of the person*. New York: Springer-Verlag.

Gladding, S. T. (1995). *Group work: A counseling specialty* (2nd ed.). Englewood Cliffs, NJ: Prentice Hall.

Hanson, P. G. (1972). What to look for in groups. In J. W. Pfeiffer & J. E. Jones (Eds.), *1972 annual handbook for group facilitators* (pp. 21-24). La Jolla, CA: University Associates.

Hicks, M. D., & Peterson, D. B. (1997). Just enough to be dangerous: The rest of what you need to know about development. *Consulting Psychology Journal: Practice and Research, 49*, 171-193.

Hill, W. F. (1969). *Learning through discussion*. Beverly Hills, CA: Sage.

Horowitz, L. (1990). *Inventory of Interpersonal Problems*. San Antonio, TX: Psychological Corporation.

Jacobs, E. E., Harvill, R. L., & Masson, R. L. (1994). *Group counseling: Strategies and skills* (2nd ed.). Pacific Grove, CA: Brooks/Cole.

Jones, J. (1973). A model of group development. In J. Jones & J. N. Pfeiffer (Eds.), *The 1973 annual handbook for group facilitators* (pp. 127-129). La Jolla, CA: University Associates.

Kees, N. L., & Jacobs, E. (1990). Conducting more effective groups: How to select and process group exercises. *Journal for Specialists in Group Work, 15*, 21-29.

Kottler, J. A., & Blau, D. S. (1989). *The imperfect therapist: Learning from failure in therapeutic practice*. San Francisco: Jossey-Bass.

Lewin, K. (1951). *Field theory in social science*. New York: Harper & Row.

MacKenzie, K. R. (1983). The clinical application of a group climate measure. In R. R. Dies & K. R. MacKenzie (Eds.), *Advances in group psychotherapy: Integrating research and practice* (pp. 159-170). New York: International Universities Press.

MacKenzie, K. R. (1997). *Time-managed group psychotherapy: Effective clinical applications*. Washington, DC: American Psychiatric Press.

MacKenzie, K. R., & Dies, R. R. (1982). *CORE battery: Clinical outcome results.* New York: American Group Psychotherapy Association.

McCafferty, D. (1997, September 12-14). The lessons of losing. *USA Weekend,* p. 20.

Monk, G., Drewery, W., & Winslade, J. (1997). Using narrative ideas in group work: A new perspective. In H. Forester-Miller & J. Kottler (Eds.), *Issues and challenges for group practitioners* (pp. 181-205). Denver, CO: Love.

Patton, M. Q. (1997). *Utilization-focused evaluation* (3rd ed.). Thousand Oaks, CA: Sage.

Pfeiffer, J., Heslin, R., & Jones, J. (Eds.). (1976). *Instrumentation in human relations training* (2nd ed.). La Jolla, CA: University Associates.

Plutchik, R., & Kellerman, H. (1974). *Emotions Profile Index.* Los Angeles: Western Psychological Services.

Rapin, L. S., & Conyne, R. K. (in press). Best practices in group counseling. In J. Trotzer (Ed.), *The counselor and the group* (3rd ed.). Muncie, IN: Accelerated Development.

Riva, M., & Kolodner, C. (Eds.). (1998). Group research: Encouraging a collaboration between practitioners and researchers [Special issue]. *Journal for Specialists in Group Work, 22*(4).

Schön, D. A. (1983). *The reflective practitioner.* New York: Basic Books.

Seligman, M. P. (1995). The effectiveness of psychotherapy: The Consumer Report study. *American Psychologist, 50,* 965-974.

Spitz, H. I. (1996). *Group psychotherapy and managed mental health care: A clinical guide for providers.* New York: Brunner/Mazel.

Sullivan, H. S. (1953). *The interpersonal theory of psychiatry.* New York: Norton.

Trotzer, J. (Ed.). (1989). *The counselor and the group* (2nd ed.). Muncie, IN: Accelerated Development.

Weissman, M. (1973). *Social Adjustment Scale—Self Report.* Princeton, NJ: Educational Testing Service Test Collection Library.

Yalom, I. D. (1975). *The theory and practice of group psychotherapy.* New York: Basic Books.

Yalom, I. D. (1995). *The theory and practice of group psychotherapy* (4th ed.). New York: Basic Books.

Index

About the Author

Robert K. Conyne, PhD, is Professor and Program Director of Counseling, University of Cincinnati. He is a graduate of Syracuse and Purdue Universities. Before joining the University of Cincinnati in 1980, he served as a counseling center psychologist and counselor educator at Illinois State University. He is a Licensed Psychologist and Clinical Counselor, a National Certified Counselor, and a Certified Group Psychotherapist. He is a Fellow of several divisions of the American Psychological Association (APA), the Association for Specialists in Group Work (ASGW), and the American Psychological Society. He is the author or coauthor of six other books, including *How Personal Growth and Task Groups Work* (Sage, 1989) and, most recently, *Comprehensive Group Work: What It Means and How to Teach It* (with F. R. Wilson and D. E. Ward), and over 150 scholarly papers and presentations in the areas of group work, prevention, and consultation. He served ASGW as journal editor for 6 years and as President (1995-96). He is currently representing both ASGW and Division 17 of APA as official liaison to China and Taiwan. In 1998, he served as a visiting scholar at the Institute of Psychology in Beijing, where he introduced task group work (as described in William Fawcett Hill's *Learning Through Discussion*) within a collaborative training and research project.

Printed in the United States
39206LVS00005B/145-162